ARL Statistics
2013–2014

Compiled and Edited by

MARTHA KYRILLIDOU
SHANEKA MORRIS
GARY ROEBUCK

ASSOCIATION OF RESEARCH LIBRARIES®
WASHINGTON, DC
2015

ARL Statistics 2013–2014

The tables presented in this publication are not indicative of performance and outcomes and should not be used as measures of library quality. In comparing any individual library to ARL medians or to other ARL members, one must be careful to make such comparisons within the context of differing institutional and local goals and characteristics.

Published by the

Association of Research Libraries®

Washington, DC 20036

www.arl.org

ISSN 0147-2135 print

ISSN 1943-5983 online

ISBN 1-59407-953-6 / 978-1-59407-953-5 print

ISBN 1-59407-954-4 / 978-1-59407-954-2 online

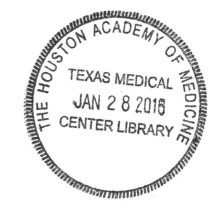

Contents

OVERVIEW

ARL Statistics 2013–2014 is the latest in a series of annual publications that describe collections, staffing, expenditures, and service activities for the 125 members of the Association of Research Libraries (ARL). Of these, 115 are university libraries; the remaining 10 are public, governmental, and nonprofit research libraries. ARL member libraries are the largest research libraries in North America, representing 17 Canadian and 108 US research institutions. The academic libraries, which comprise 92% of the membership, include 16 Canadian and 99 US libraries.

Statistics have been collected and published annually for the members of the Association of Research Libraries since 1961–62, and the data are available through an interactive web interface. Prior to 1961–62, annual statistics for university libraries were collected by James Gerould, first at the University of Minnesota and later at Princeton University.[1] These data, covering the years 1907–08 through 1961–62, are now called the Gerould statistics.[2] The whole data series from 1908, which is available on the ARL Statistics website at http://arlstatistics.org/publications, represents the oldest and most comprehensive continuing library statistical series in North America.

ARL libraries are a relatively small subset of libraries in North America, but they do account for a large portion of academic library resources in terms of assets, budgets, and the number of users they serve. The total library expenditures of all 125 member libraries in 2013–2014 was almost $4.7 billion; from that, approximately $3.4 billion was spent by the 115 university libraries and more than $1.2 billion by the nonuniversity libraries. The pie charts below show how the two types of libraries divide these expenditures differently.

University Libraries 2013–2014

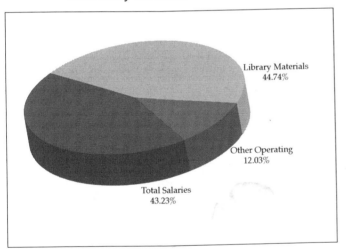

Library Materials
44.74%

Other Operating
12.03%

Total Salaries
43.23%

Nonuniversity Libraries 2013–2014

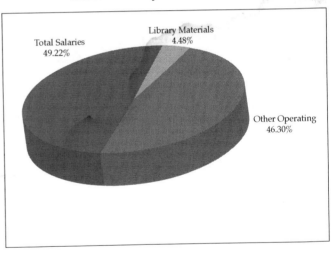

Total Salaries
49.22%

Library Materials
4.48%

Other Operating
46.30%

1 Kendon L. Stubbs and Robert E. Molyneux, *Research Library Statistics 1907–08 through 1987–88.* (Washington, DC: ARL, 1990).

2 Robert E. Molyneux, *The Gerould Statistics 1907/08 – 1961/62.* (Washington, DC: ARL, 1986) http://www.libqual.org/documents/admin/2012/1986_Molyneux_Gerould.pdf and http://www.libqual.org/documents/admin/2012/2010_Molyneux_Gerould.pdf

ARL Statistics® Analytics

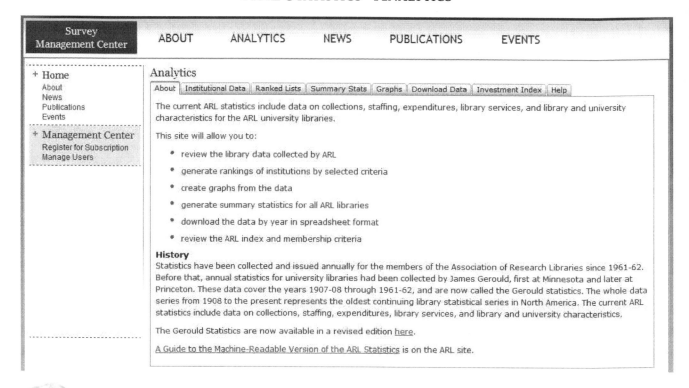

ARL now offers interactive access to over 100 years' worth of ARL Statistics® data through the **ARL Statistics® Analytics** interface (formerly called ARL Statistics® Interactive Analytics). Subscribers also have access to the ARL Statistics Publications database and the mailings archive, which contains instructions, definitions, and supportive documentation for the annual survey data collection. Libraries that are not ARL members, for-profit and not-for-profit entities, and individual researchers may subscribe to password access to this Excel-based data set. The annual subscription fee is $500 for non-profit organizations and $750 for all others. Customers may contact <stats@arl.org> for subscription information or place an order through their subscription agent.

Subscribers may download Excel files containing the entire data set or any combination of survey years and variables. They may also create graphs and ranked lists of the data through the interactive interface.

Note: PDFs of the *ARL Statistics, ARL Academic Health Sciences Library Statistics,* and *ARL Academic Law Library Statistics* publications are not included in this service.

We would like to thank the University of Virginia for supporting the ARL Statistics Interactive edition from 1995 to 2010. Special thanks to Texas A&M University and the University of Texas for enabling ARL to support data curation activities like the ARL Statistics® Analytics through their support and development of LibQUAL+® Analytics.

ARL LIBRARY DATA TABLES

2013–2014

COLLECTIONS AND COLLECTION EXPENDITURES

	Notes	Titles Held 1	Volumes In Library 2	Electronic Books 4	One-time resource purchases 7a	Ongoing resource purchases 7b	Collection Support 7c	Total Library Materials 7
ALABAMA	LMb+	3,841,736	4,391,464	1,225,058	1,899,035	8,449,837	538,136	10,887,008
ALBERTA	LM+	4,463,667	8,398,944	1,161,675	6,260,034	11,959,233	1,524,426	19,743,693
ARIZONA	LMb+	4,796,552	6,877,849	1,522,548	3,087,253	10,414,308	1,159,417	14,660,978
ARIZONA STATE	LB+	3,961,127	4,669,306	584,430	1,978,479	9,716,725	428,294	12,123,498
AUBURN	b+	3,492,354	4,416,728	867,928	587,794	5,986,779	20,045	6,594,618
BOSTON	LMb+	2,924,255	3,688,478	1,259,861	1,541,266	9,764,918	284,349	11,590,533
BOSTON COLLEGE	Lb+	2,463,662	3,174,742	570,918	2,766,541	8,872,359	263,601	11,902,501
BRIGHAM YOUNG	L+	4,016,365	4,633,306	717,939	2,089,952	8,571,836	300,202	10,961,990
BRITISH COLUMBIA	LMb+	5,698,583	6,631,545	1,843,028	4,498,091	12,122,295	142,741	16,763,126
BROWN	Mb+	4,161,965	5,415,232	1,607,045	3,757,453	6,781,251	973,055	11,511,759
CALGARY	LM+	3,165,928	3,945,194	944,517	2,233,735	8,708,524	1,198,261	12,140,520
CALIFORNIA, BERKELEY	Lb+	10,114,791	12,548,223	1,534,101	7,148,257	14,979,072	599,463	22,726,792
CALIFORNIA, DAVIS	LMb+	3,401,755	4,510,293	705,993	1,453,947	7,437,406	49,305	8,940,658
CALIFORNIA, IRVINE	LMb+	3,155,263	3,430,327	1,004,187	2,026,190	7,087,710	204,424	9,318,324
CALIFORNIA, LOS ANGELES	LM+	11,898,411	12,007,941	1,722,087	4,779,798	9,973,207	857,460	15,610,465
CALIFORNIA, RIVERSIDE	+	2,663,262	4,134,518	640,591	626,387	3,546,179	251,976	4,424,542
CALIFORNIA, SAN DIEGO	M+	4,713,846	5,583,014	1,784,849	2,544,286	7,021,984	0	9,566,270
CALIFORNIA, SANTA BARBARA	+	8,046,138	3,123,554	652,970	1,487,400	4,126,733	246,673	5,860,806
CASE WESTERN RESERVE	LMb+	2,527,723	3,173,419	549,840	1,129,652	6,426,490	100,781	7,656,923
CHICAGO	LMb+	6,860,280	11,560,575	1,407,239	5,813,318	12,869,225	494,110	19,176,653
CINCINNATI	LMBb+	3,484,607	4,473,475	1,431,414	1,536,369	8,385,381	255,915	10,177,665
COLORADO	b+	5,404,282	7,641,471	584,830	2,100,368	8,241,720	858,278	11,200,366
COLORADO STATE	b+	1,885,182	2,245,807	479,338	578,482	6,549,395	695,649	7,823,526
COLUMBIA	LM+	9,022,370	13,119,661	1,952,798	9,488,655	17,004,556	3,006,838	29,500,049
CONNECTICUT	LMBb+	2,641,242	3,923,364	564,181	1,173,873	8,372,512	1,146,923	10,693,308
CORNELL	LMB+	6,948,123	9,198,958	1,173,921	.	.	.	21,560,997
DARTMOUTH	Mb+	2,829,616	3,363,205	731,574	1,665,811	8,800,071	229,239	10,695,121
DELAWARE	+	2,253,730	3,235,685	422,284	2,671,457	7,479,184	319,232	10,469,873
DUKE	LMb+	5,898,837	7,607,727	1,392,485	6,308,215	11,908,356	503,804	18,720,375
EMORY	LMB+	3,378,987	4,184,484	688,935	5,277,854	12,374,707	45,080	17,697,641

COLLECTIONS AND COLLECTION EXPENDITURES

	Notes	Titles Held 1	Volumes In Library 2	Electronic Books 4	One-time resource purchases 7a	Ongoing resource purchases 7b	Collection Support 7c	Total Library Materials 7
FLORIDA	LMBb+	4,933,357	5,021,000	1,152,307	1,022,641	11,271,840	533,500	12,827,981
FLORIDA STATE	LMBb+	3,067,049	2,836,043	357,153	1,107,346	8,141,374	192,214	9,440,934
GEORGE WASHINGTON	LMB+	2,314,270	3,134,858	619,713	2,483,411	7,942,201	1,767,410	12,193,022
GEORGETOWN	LMBb+	4,055,631	4,798,606	1,672,222	3,878,430	10,150,007	370,985	14,399,422
GEORGIA	Lb+	4,024,380	5,089,626	623,448	2,300,116	9,818,449	713,126	12,831,691
GEORGIA TECH	+	1,098,890	2,489,518	272,503	329,325	7,145,229	0	7,474,554
GUELPH	B+	1,847,444	2,021,024	408,669	1,493,172	4,865,533	802,009	7,160,715
HARVARD	LMb+	14,195,095	19,848,652	710,029	18,203,127	17,014,186	9,636,705	44,854,018
HAWAII	LMb+	2,895,212	3,466,292	272,949	1,167,982	6,455,646	232,860	7,856,488
HOUSTON	Lb+	2,516,360	3,352,322	612,230	1,042,641	9,153,224	1,223,383	11,419,248
HOWARD	LMb+	1,352,528	2,947,284	170,703	258,156	4,838,729	673,065	5,769,950
ILLINOIS, CHICAGO	Mb+	2,534,801	2,315,361	455,617	1,040,969	7,001,547	11,402	8,053,918
ILLINOIS, URBANA	Lb+	8,383,821	14,072,988	903,279	5,624,045	12,949,625	639,031	19,212,701
INDIANA	L+	7,234,398	9,934,302	1,864,483	5,722,628	9,720,125	585,035	16,027,788
IOWA	LM+	5,376,505	7,311,554	1,578,459	3,070,277	14,878,228	654,753	18,603,258
IOWA STATE	+	2,421,622	2,858,602	384,019	2,436,681	11,103,006	216,960	13,756,647
JOHNS HOPKINS	MB+	3,731,332	4,460,406	1,210,320	3,041,280	15,150,497	304,608	18,496,385
KANSAS	LMBb+	4,813,780	4,693,070	911,465	1,955,354	7,697,432	478,933	10,131,719
KENT STATE	+	2,559,662	3,316,723	910,201	725,616	4,028,731	626,734	5,381,081
KENTUCKY	LMb+	3,501,066	4,608,331	1,127,500	1,473,797	8,747,061	755,785	10,976,643
LAVAL	LM+	2,036,697	4,180,577	202,901	2,747,635	8,807,432	397,679	11,952,746
LOUISIANA STATE	LMb+	5,125,306	5,038,796	704,715	921,941	6,139,559	146,999	7,208,499
LOUISVILLE	MBb+	1,660,906	2,332,386	60,930	260,948	9,440,879	223,002	9,924,829
MCGILL	LMBb+	4,392,826	5,486,918	1,830,225	4,102,120	12,555,101	0	16,657,221
MCMASTER	Mb+	1,997,052	2,253,025	589,717	751,491	7,392,295	968,007	9,111,792
MANITOBA	LMb+	2,085,532	2,519,848	723,400	2,226,359	6,533,880	645,319	9,405,558
MARYLAND	b+	3,909,206	4,328,653	1,031,379	1,811,482	8,932,868	655,798	11,400,148
MASSACHUSETTS	+	3,310,591	4,351,859	1,632,455	1,179,430	6,143,647	248,384	7,571,461
MIT	b+	2,192,182	2,881,988	576,107	1,368,982	8,252,796	254,257	9,876,035
MIAMI	LMb+	3,105,352	3,610,359	793,492	2,624,821	10,387,381	267,958	13,280,160

COLLECTIONS AND COLLECTION EXPENDITURES

	Notes	Titles Held 1	Volumes In Library 2	Electronic Books 4	One-time resource purchases 7a	Ongoing resource purchases 7b	Collection Support 7c	Total Library Materials 7
MICHIGAN	LM+	8,690,613	13,250,648	2,524,792	8,140,507	15,228,888	2,089,726	25,459,121
MICHIGAN STATE	L+	6,695,099	6,721,988	1,594,547	3,905,692	11,773,745	629,535	16,308,972
MINNESOTA	LMb+	4,034,731	8,256,400	595,029	3,960,427	13,229,303	773,932	17,963,662
MISSOURI	LM+	3,610,590	4,682,304	1,467,268	1,036,556	7,314,620	309,499	8,660,675
MONTREAL	LMb+	2,857,474	3,814,783	580,671	2,061,115	10,147,750	301,741	12,510,606
NEBRASKA	Lb+	2,700,142	3,791,910	760,450	1,324,811	7,228,018	65,885	8,618,714
NEW MEXICO	LMb+	3,973,114	3,389,401	691,932	1,249,463	6,533,881	1,558,287	9,341,631
NEW YORK	LMBb+	5,304,562	6,253,028	1,749,379	10,455,721	15,840,884	979,211	27,275,816
NORTH CAROLINA	LM+	4,877,368	7,814,952	1,219,543	4,696,643	10,634,400	226,321	15,557,364
NORTH CAROLINA STATE	+	2,551,636	4,919,705	761,640	1,398,786	7,997,862	1,282,563	10,679,211
NORTHWESTERN	LMBb+	5,286,321	6,251,124	1,416,083	4,186,625	11,037,394	478,454	15,702,473
NOTRE DAME	Lb+	3,734,225	4,591,712	667,466	5,126,375	7,854,164	371,765	13,352,304
OHIO	MBb+	3,035,871	3,386,986	1,026,826	708,603	4,062,419	222,659	4,993,681
OHIO STATE	LMb+	6,075,215	8,926,559	858,294	5,860,676	12,109,129	1,008,109	18,977,914
OKLAHOMA	LM+	3,939,771	6,116,152	1,288,785	2,281,125	11,194,632	823,272	14,299,029
OKLAHOMA STATE	MBb+	3,438,141	4,104,776	1,623,854	1,743,796	6,925,037	213,721	8,882,554
OREGON	LBb+	2,145,929	3,245,882	298,281	1,699,747	5,478,150	265,795	7,443,692
OTTAWA	LM+	2,565,867	3,360,829	1,030,312	5,579,453	8,369,180	10,482	13,959,115
PENNSYLVANIA	LM	5,337,449	7,410,549	1,150,462	4,380,540	13,200,409	804,532	18,385,481
PENNSYLVANIA STATE	LMBb+	5,336,986	7,281,750	444,358	5,135,616	14,539,358	612,749	20,287,723
PITTSBURGH	LMB+	5,218,300	7,124,077	1,269,457	2,096,485	13,815,011	705,799	16,617,295
PRINCETON	b+	6,257,295	8,663,694	382,935	11,562,978	13,172,616	1,101,417	25,837,011
PURDUE	+	2,587,047	3,747,273	1,569,477	1,782,128	11,263,563	383,222	13,428,913
QUEEN'S	LMb+	2,622,287	3,119,094	684,259	1,018,314	7,251,449	652,217	8,921,980
RICE	+	2,407,628	2,842,929	122,516	2,381,832	7,104,980	459,251	9,946,063
ROCHESTER	Mb+	3,087,086	4,207,872	585,301	2,206,724	7,653,434	84,134	9,944,292
RUTGERS	LBM+	3,146,048	5,455,299	687,898	1,198,053	12,753,158	159,154	14,110,365
SASKATCHEWAN	LM+	1,919,329	2,669,043	518,154	1,868,872	9,426,502	413,111	11,708,485
SOUTH CAROLINA	LMb+	2,489,688	5,679,527	619,459	571,537	8,109,377	260,996	8,941,910
SOUTHERN CALIFORNIA	LMBb+	3,991,257	5,571,398	1,054,103	4,928,267	17,024,865	475,784	22,428,916

Collections and Collection Expenditures

	Notes	Titles Held 1	Volumes In Library 2	Electronic Books 4	One-time resource purchases 7a	Ongoing resource purchases 7b	Collection Support 7c	Total Library Materials 7
SOUTHERN ILLINOIS	LM+	2,315,485	3,360,046	268,365	718,528	5,760,870	468,842	6,948,240
SUNY-ALBANY	b+	1,602,005	2,511,510	123,776	713,016	5,024,993	295,082	6,033,091
SUNY-BUFFALO	LM+	3,646,471	4,130,967	726,272	1,012,545	7,987,314	65,468	9,065,327
SUNY-STONY BROOK	Mb+	2,182,148	2,209,471	351,199	602,464	7,444,594	354,563	8,401,621
SYRACUSE	Lb+	3,041,584	4,039,493	317,214	2,078,121	7,216,767	275,666	9,570,554
TEMPLE	LMBb+	3,446,686	4,584,591	906,720	2,063,849	9,060,269	387,192	11,511,310
TENNESSEE	LMBb+	2,494,291	3,522,904	587,530	1,770,715	12,651,455	359,007	14,781,177
TEXAS	L+	7,095,417	11,393,355	1,201,996	9,356,911	11,104,352	461,386	20,922,649
TEXAS A&M	MBLb+	4,109,075	5,173,340	1,509,470	3,771,490	16,572,497	3,265,093	23,609,080
TEXAS TECH	LMB+	796,729	3,478,869	631,240	1,378,641	12,775,717	102,283	14,256,641
TORONTO	LMB+	8,041,704	13,923,039	1,905,362	12,918,674	16,332,058	473,956	29,724,687
TULANE	LMB+	2,976,484	4,479,101	1,010,105	2,495,847	8,734,433	683,326	11,913,606
UTAH	LMb+	3,448,961	3,671,129	345,663	2,063,230	6,404,157	328,848	8,796,235
VANDERBILT	LM+	3,861,552	4,614,805	1,535,056	1,082,273	10,709,846	158,182	11,950,301
VIRGINIA	LMb+	5,197,490	5,655,334	501,605	2,825,419	9,104,526	179,175	12,109,120
VIRGINIA TECH	b+	2,279,339	3,147,160	816,733	1,678,319	6,870,496	612,201	9,161,016
WASHINGTON	LMBb+	.	9,463,768	619,007	3,606,697	11,375,014	1,086,283	16,067,994
WASHINGTON STATE	Bb+	2,378,138	2,946,984	589,564	559,020	6,288,664	0	6,847,684
WASHINGTON U.-ST. LOUIS	LMb+	4,006,376	5,128,983	1,494,508	2,755,186	10,685,631	270,621	13,711,438
WATERLOO	+	2,361,400	2,487,344	416,952	898,998	7,677,094	288,190	8,864,282
WAYNE STATE	LMb+	2,583,935	2,976,886	927,462	520,680	8,724,568	218,242	9,463,490
WESTERN	Lb+	3,886,093	5,271,741	1,307,420	1,754,437	10,863,422	671,965	13,289,824
WISCONSIN	LM+	7,437,916	9,575,506	1,178,742	3,143,151	9,177,031	476,884	12,797,066
YALE	LMb+	10,695,257	13,547,882	1,456,769	24,036,092	13,384,956	1,362,835	38,783,883
YORK	LB+	3,348,325	4,325,241	1,231,317	3,115,527	7,779,172	100,682	10,995,381
BOSTON PUBLIC	b+	3,235,442	4,341,961	50,720	4,056,585	407,000	.	4,463,585
NATL RES COUNCIL CANADA	b+	.	.	.	.	.	.	.
CENTER FOR RESEARCH LIBS	+	.	.	.	.	1,209,670	24,760	1,234,430
LIBRARY OF CONGRESS	LBb+	128,923,299	39,156,157	1,041,000	15,088,019	9,451,917	0	24,539,936
NATL AGRICULTURAL LIB	+	1,171,277	2,402,664	65,763	275,240	4,931,236	262,520	5,468,996

COLLECTIONS AND COLLECTION EXPENDITURES

	Notes	Titles Held 1	Volumes In Library 2	Electronic Books 4	One-time resource purchases 7a	Ongoing resource purchases 7b	Collection Support 7c	Total Library Materials 7
NATL ARCHIVES	+	105,400	186,770	0	2,000	82,000	22,000	106,000
NATL LIB OF MEDICINE	+	1,476,641	2,781,201	14,686	1,283,409	1,092,601	790,108	3,166,118
NEW YORK PUBLIC	+	7,956,702	10,417,846	407,897	7,887,569	4,659,089	205,342	12,752,000
NEW YORK STATE		2,037,870	2,874,214	10,530	142,551	1,997,160	0	2,139,711
SMITHSONIAN	+	885,926	2,006,334	0	406,470	1,429,689	375,770	2,211,929

+ - See Footnotes
L - Includes Law Library
M - Includes Medical Library

B - Includes branch campuses
b - Basis of volume count is bibliographic
. - Unavailable, not applicable or no data supplied

COLLECTIONS AND COLLECTION EXPENDITURES
Summary Data

		Titles Held 1	Volumes In Library 2	Electronic Books 4	One-time resource purchases 7a	Ongoing resource purchases 7b	Collection Support 7c	Total Library Materials 7
University Libraries	Mean	4,087,170	5,418,614	932,998	3,125,872	9,513,812	628,008	13,339,807
	Median	3,466,784	4,460,406	793,492	2,070,985	8,803,752	405,395	11,708,485
	High	14,195,095	19,848,652	2,524,792	24,036,092	17,024,865	9,636,705	44,854,018
	Low	796,729	2,021,024	60,930	258,156	3,546,179	0	4,424,542
	Totals	465,937,422	623,140,553	107,294,732	356,349,450	1,084,574,536	71,592,873	1,534,077,856
	Number of Libraries Reporting	114	115	115	114	114	114	115
Nonuniversity Libraries	Median	1,757,256	2,827,708	32,703	844,940	1,429,689	115,051	3,166,118
	Totals	145,792,557	64,167,147	1,590,596	29,141,843	25,260,362	1,680,500	56,082,705
	Number of Libraries Reporting	8	8	8	8	9	8	9
Grand Totals		611,729,979	687,307,700	108,885,328	385,491,293	1,109,834,898	73,273,373	1,590,160,561

Salary Expenditures

	Notes	Salaries & Wages Professional Staff 8a	Salaries & Wages Support Staff 8b	Salaries & Wages Student Assistants 8c	Total Salaries and Wages 8	Fringe Benefits 10	Fringe Benefits - designated % 11
ALABAMA	LMb+	5,246,628	2,041,538	559,171	7,847,337	2,215,796	32.00
ALBERTA	LM+	7,295,214	6,966,718	627,510	14,889,441	3,290,361	.
ARIZONA	LMb+	5,255,513	4,488,078	717,535	10,461,126	3,636,592	30.00
ARIZONA STATE	LB+	3,952,263	5,421,125	561,727	9,935,115	3,587,778	37.00
AUBURN	b+	3,309,189	960,700	439,384	4,709,273	1,323,666	31.00
BOSTON	LMb+	6,701,855	3,536,329	616,022	10,854,206	2,791,044	29.80
BOSTON COLLEGE	Lb+	6,174,748	2,928,874	826,735	9,930,357	3,404,531	38.00
BRIGHAM YOUNG	L+	8,294,259	2,234,939	2,930,564	13,459,762	6,990,158	64.60
BRITISH COLUMBIA	LMb+	10,370,898	6,067,911	1,288,854	17,727,662	3,237,608	17.00
BROWN	Mb+	5,420,337	3,670,593	333,038	9,423,968	2,778,527	30.50
CALGARY	LM+	6,401,274	8,372,103	593,763	15,367,141	3,306,255	20.00
CALIFORNIA, BERKELEY	Lb+	18,460,866	5,878,383	2,641,663	26,980,912	9,347,203	.
CALIFORNIA, DAVIS	LMb+	4,640,356	4,083,866	436,594	9,160,816	4,325,953	48.00
CALIFORNIA, IRVINE	LMb+	4,758,552	4,914,961	462,279	10,135,792	4,053,696	.
CALIFORNIA, LOS ANGELES	LM+	13,955,356	11,146,934	2,625,932	27,728,222	10,085,906	.
CALIFORNIA, RIVERSIDE	+	2,885,792	2,573,599	386,557	5,845,948	2,485,707	32.00
CALIFORNIA, SAN DIEGO	M+	8,535,459	4,356,666	1,205,843	14,097,968	6,862,614	49.00
CALIFORNIA, SANTA BARBARA	+	3,618,814	4,049,814	767,534	8,436,162	3,181,411	26.50
CASE WESTERN RESERVE	LMb+	3,824,019	1,107,552	562,970	5,494,541	1,553,445	31.50
CHICAGO	LMb+	5,809,150	6,791,294	1,205,749	13,806,193	3,721,968	29.50
CINCINNATI	LMBb+	6,289,936	1,734,838	712,295	8,737,069	3,287,552	41.10
COLORADO	b+	3,971,369	4,268,649	1,004,849	9,244,867	2,468,865	28.00
COLORADO STATE	b+	3,907,093	2,740,512	787,078	7,434,683	2,679,425	25.00
COLUMBIA	LM+	22,882,142	7,211,579	1,513,342	31,607,063	10,420,950	33.70
CONNECTICUT	LMBb+	6,680,551	3,771,518	480,468	10,932,537	5,791,803	55.00
CORNELL	LMB+	15,157,396	8,026,063	803,183	23,986,642	6,776,599	36.00
DARTMOUTH	Mb+	4,832,136	3,764,601	465,323	9,062,060	2,957,493	34.50
DELAWARE	+	4,861,867	2,880,513	367,963	8,110,343	3,608,263	36.20
DUKE	LMb+	11,248,612	4,562,933	30,190	15,841,735	4,050,652	26.30
EMORY	LMB+	9,993,130	5,321,254	851,374	16,165,758	3,960,113	28.00

SALARY EXPENDITURES

	Notes	Salaries & Wages Professional Staff 8a	Salaries & Wages Support Staff 8b	Salaries & Wages Student Assistants 8c	Total Salaries and Wages 8	Fringe Benefits 10	Fringe Benefits - designated % 11
FLORIDA	LMBb+	6,410,523	6,651,793	581,107	13,643,423	4,308,200	26.00
FLORIDA STATE	LMBb+	4,915,145	2,071,530	869,056	7,855,731	2,152,947	28.00
GEORGE WASHINGTON	LMB+	6,377,747	4,866,590	642,882	11,887,219	2,956,158	25.00
GEORGETOWN	LMBb+	7,665,092	4,261,612	762,290	12,688,994	4,204,894	38.00
GEORGIA	Lb+	4,631,630	5,224,787	881,948	10,738,365	3,442,705	34.00
GEORGIA TECH	+	3,618,001	2,775,438	78,781	6,472,220	1,805,106	28.50
GUELPH	B+	4,499,047	2,634,206	173,846	7,307,099	2,063,056	28.20
HARVARD	LMb+	39,722,648	16,563,134	2,827,890	59,113,672	26,344,845	34.10
HAWAII	LMb+	6,211,010	2,675,965	1,081,750	9,968,725	4,023,931	45.46
HOUSTON	Lb+	4,397,957	2,530,151	658,041	7,586,149	2,324,576	31.00
HOWARD	LMb+	2,551,774	2,034,052	175,394	4,761,220	1,022,477	29.10
ILLINOIS, CHICAGO	Mb+	4,426,334	3,001,907	683,847	8,112,088	3,110,986	38.35
ILLINOIS, URBANA	Lb+	12,388,327	7,496,010	2,665,449	22,549,786	8,600,406	44.67
INDIANA	L+	9,039,138	4,171,963	1,590,671	14,801,772	5,687,766	43.72
IOWA	LM+	6,625,088	4,425,883	832,327	11,883,298	4,370,311	35.00
IOWA STATE	+	2,595,348	3,965,009	382,433	6,942,790	2,508,881	.
JOHNS HOPKINS	MB+	9,916,909	3,460,201	697,595	14,074,705	4,304,227	34.50
KANSAS	LMBb+	7,707,214	2,311,884	917,065	10,936,163	3,385,709	18.76
KENT STATE	+	3,467,002	715,312	542,743	4,725,057	1,687,043	35.00
KENTUCKY	LMb+	5,941,463	2,258,765	508,814	8,709,042	2,595,972	27.00
LAVAL	LM+	4,333,449	5,898,039	.	10,231,488	2,685,267	19.70
LOUISIANA STATE	LMb+	3,474,679	1,873,429	485,290	5,833,398	2,012,739	40.00
LOUISVILLE	MBb+	3,307,333	2,449,004	480,163	6,236,500	2,152,531	28.00
MCGILL	LMBb+	5,148,517	6,558,930	245,596	11,953,042	1,945,687	28.00
MCMASTER	Mb+	3,475,708	2,826,783	228,107	6,530,598	2,567,072	42.00
MANITOBA	LMb+	5,576,316	4,897,713	825,832	11,299,862	2,244,853	18.00
MARYLAND	b+	8,958,676	2,722,251	951,643	12,632,570	3,576,233	.
MASSACHUSETTS	+	4,828,484	3,036,092	719,850	8,584,426	213,164	28.30
MIT	b+	7,281,943	2,735,104	433,327	10,450,374	2,804,055	28.00
MIAMI	LMb+	6,272,753	3,354,294	658,353	10,285,400	3,238,297	.

SALARY EXPENDITURES

	Notes	Salaries & Wages Professional Staff 8a	Salaries & Wages Support Staff 8b	Salaries & Wages Student Assistants 8c	Total Salaries and Wages 8	Fringe Benefits 10	Fringe Benefits - designated % 11
MICHIGAN	LM+	15,317,578	16,373,733	2,230,905	33,922,216	10,173,954	32.00
MICHIGAN STATE	L+	6,429,186	5,480,278	746,319	12,655,783		
MINNESOTA	LMb+	8,717,959	8,583,337	1,352,313	18,653,609	6,207,554	34.90
MISSOURI	LM+	3,626,076	3,100,354	471,597	7,198,027	2,267,319	35.37
MONTREAL	LMb+	8,540,463	9,680,096	145,278	18,365,838	4,938,220	
NEBRASKA	Lb+	3,444,989	3,182,712	690,447	7,318,148	1,999,139	28.30
NEW MEXICO	LMb+	4,043,802	4,713,181	776,856	9,533,839	2,937,832	32.28
NEW YORK	LMBb+	16,276,117	6,482,542	1,147,501	23,906,160	6,976,140	35.40
NORTH CAROLINA	LM+	10,114,220	7,534,638	1,083,048	18,731,906	5,267,232	22.04
NORTH CAROLINA STATE	+	8,886,377	3,690,822	892,505	13,469,704	3,788,530	30.00
NORTHWESTERN	LMBb+	9,334,496	5,172,863	757,768	15,265,127	3,874,164	27.20
NOTRE DAME	Lb+	7,035,684	3,671,429	476,433	11,183,546	3,626,447	26.70
OHIO	MBb+	2,655,064	1,878,021	531,757	5,064,842	1,678,343	36.60
OHIO STATE	LMb+	11,027,225	6,757,247	2,005,589	19,790,061	5,614,821	31.00
OKLAHOMA	LM+	4,244,788	2,362,779	1,273,742	7,881,309	2,161,473	35.00
OKLAHOMA STATE	MBb+	3,692,870	2,177,038	819,183	6,689,091	2,205,656	40.16
OREGON	LBb+	5,111,226	3,532,482	1,345,604	9,989,312	5,009,065	50.00
OTTAWA	LM+	4,274,665	5,122,335	201,213	9,598,213	2,575,527	
PENNSYLVANIA	LM	10,626,168	8,290,025	1,704,859	20,621,052	6,552,938	34.10
PENNSYLVANIA STATE	LMBb+	12,510,157	13,570,304	478,130	26,558,591	8,856,490	39.80
PITTSBURGH	LMB+	6,959,231	4,439,516	706,661	12,105,408	4,405,666	38.90
PRINCETON	b+	11,596,949	7,900,908	1,254,277	20,752,134	5,440,438	28.00
PURDUE	+	5,610,520	2,454,434	917,446	8,982,400	3,617,843	34.00
QUEEN'S	LMb+	3,876,160	3,369,417	335,818	7,581,395	1,787,666	
RICE	+	4,143,170	1,280,527	155,316	5,579,013	1,536,300	28.00
ROCHESTER	Mb+	5,556,340	2,004,751	550,425	8,111,516	2,555,129	31.00
RUTGERS	LBM+	9,553,395	12,846,219	1,516,930	23,916,544	9,212,188	49.85
SASKATCHEWAN	LM+	5,360,259	3,595,234	367,843	9,323,336	1,441,389	
SOUTH CAROLINA	LMb+	4,761,611	3,051,112	841,639	8,654,362	2,599,429	33.00
SOUTHERN CALIFORNIA	LMBb+	11,365,209	5,628,427	1,769,510	18,763,146	5,856,332	33.50

Salary Expenditures

	Notes	Salaries & Wages Professional Staff 8a	Salaries & Wages Support Staff 8b	Salaries & Wages Student Assistants 8c	Total Salaries and Wages 8	Fringe Benefits 10	Fringe Benefits - designated % 11
SOUTHERN ILLINOIS	LM+	2,503,379	2,118,529	670,502	5,292,410	2,283,886	55.00
SUNY-ALBANY	b+	4,143,535	1,310,831	459,342	5,913,708	2,966,316	50.16
SUNY-BUFFALO	LM+	7,024,887	1,807,503	658,134	9,490,524	5,132,848	58.75
SUNY-STONY BROOK	Mb+	3,885,449	547,157	399,053	4,831,659	.	.
SYRACUSE	Lb+	6,717,298	2,033,337	324,461	9,075,096	3,291,401	41.00
TEMPLE	LMBb+	5,951,659	1,989,200	751,883	8,692,742	2,374,882	33.00
TENNESSEE	LMBb+	5,956,510	3,699,107	564,185	10,219,802	2,866,679	20.00
TEXAS	L+	9,803,866	10,799,408	1,713,942	22,317,216	4,790,843	32.00
TEXAS A&M	MBLb+	9,387,531	3,983,357	905,163	14,276,051	380,638	28.00
TEXAS TECH	LMB+	5,663,728	5,055,463	1,091,758	11,810,949	3,371,847	29.00
TORONTO	LMB+	15,986,078	17,409,156	4,150,072	37,545,305	8,889,647	24.75
TULANE	LMB+	3,661,025	2,451,867	231,727	6,344,619	1,411,898	24.00
UTAH	LMb+	5,595,744	5,803,506	1,513,528	12,912,778	4,936,529	42.00
VANDERBILT	LM+	6,479,461	2,909,667	583,520	9,972,648	2,350,260	26.00
VIRGINIA	LMb+	9,972,423	6,314,097	766,975	17,053,495	5,260,949	24.90
VIRGINIA TECH	b+	3,832,504	2,935,571	372,054	7,140,129	2,228,120	28.50
WASHINGTON	LMBb+	12,353,732	6,710,696	1,777,453	20,841,881	6,358,734	30.90
WASHINGTON STATE	Bb+	2,847,144	2,820,858	537,115	6,205,117	1,966,729	.
WASHINGTON U.-ST. LOUIS	LMb+	6,408,407	3,270,228	529,492	10,208,127	3,639,059	30.00
WATERLOO	+	2,694,247	3,889,946	828,130	7,412,323	1,644,727	21.00
WAYNE STATE	LMb+	5,866,861	943,122	934,803	7,744,786	1,972,008	26.80
WESTERN	Lb+	4,946,946	3,821,934	231,942	9,000,822	2,388,209	27.50
WISCONSIN	LM+	14,072,915	4,129,500	2,665,963	20,868,378	.	.
YALE	LMb+	21,027,999	16,127,870	817,458	37,973,327	14,657,836	29.40
YORK	LB+	6,930,869	4,996,613	941,381	12,868,863	2,806,294	.
BOSTON PUBLIC	b+	.	.	.	24,181,779	6,154,263	25.45
NATL RES COUNCIL CANADA	b+	.	.	.	.	.	.
CENTER FOR RESEARCH LIBS	+	2,123,927	515,994	204,949	2,844,870	962,190	.
LIBRARY OF CONGRESS	LBb+	.	.	.	314,195,170	94,258,551	30.00
NATL AGRICULTURAL LIB	+	8,991,757	1,690,325	0	10,682,082	3,738,729	35.00

Salary Expenditures

	Notes	Salaries & Wages Professional Staff 8a	Salaries & Wages Support Staff 8b	Salaries & Wages Student Assistants 8c	Total Salaries and Wages 8	Fringe Benefits 10	Fringe Benefits - designated % 11
NATL ARCHIVES	+	40,294,748	137,889,212	4,294,866	182,478,826	0	36.45
NATL LIB OF MEDICINE	+	19,622,003	2,751,337	234,177	22,607,517	6,688,675	28.00
NEW YORK PUBLIC	+	.	.	.	47,244,000	27,309,000	.
NEW YORK STATE		2,311,908	1,899,572	175,700	4,387,180	2,336,529	55.48
SMITHSONIAN	+	6,138,562	1,679,690	0	7,818,252	2,303,058	30.00

+ - See Footnotes
L - Includes Law Library
M - Includes Medical Library

B - Includes branch campuses
b - Basis of volume count is bibliographic
. - Unavailable, not applicable or no data supplied

SALARY EXPENDITURES
Summary Data

		Salaries & Wages Professional Staff 8a	Salaries & Wages Support Staff 8b	Salaries & Wages Student Assistants 8c	Total Salaries and Wages 8	Fringe Benefits 10	Fringe Benefits - designated % 11
University Libraries	Mean	7,294,836	4,714,153	889,075	12,890,333	4,068,354	33.09
	Median	5,951,659	3,771,518	714,915	10,219,802	3,288,957	31.00
	High	39,722,648	17,409,156	4,150,072	59,113,672	26,344,845	64.60
	Low	2,503,379	547,157	30,190	4,709,273	213,164	17.00
	Totals	838,906,178	542,127,552	101,354,528	1,482,388,259	455,655,592	
	Number of Libraries Reporting	115	115	114	115	112	99
Nonuniversity Libraries	Median	7,565,160	1,794,949	190,325	22,607,517	4,946,496	30.00
	Totals	79,482,905	146,426,130	4,909,692	616,439,676	143,750,995	
	Number of Libraries Reporting	6	6	6	9	8	7
Grand Totals		918,389,083	688,553,682	106,264,220	2,098,827,935	599,406,587	

Overall Expenditures

	Notes	Total Library Materials 7	Total Salaries and Wages 8	Other Operating Expenditures 9	Total Library Expenditures 6	Bibl. Utilities, Networks, etc. External Expenditures 12
ALABAMA	LMb+	10,887,008	7,847,337	1,655,547	20,389,892	39,668
ALBERTA	LM+	19,743,693	14,889,441	3,533,440	38,166,575	.
ARIZONA	LMb+	14,660,978	10,461,126	3,644,219	28,766,323	622,398
ARIZONA STATE	LB+	12,123,498	9,935,115	2,806,112	24,864,725	.
AUBURN	b+	6,594,618	4,709,273	1,214,482	12,518,373	30,056
BOSTON	LMb+	11,590,533	10,854,206	2,214,384	24,659,123	989,825
BOSTON COLLEGE	Lb+	11,902,501	9,930,357	1,277,431	23,110,289	97,226
BRIGHAM YOUNG	L+	10,961,990	13,459,762	3,059,592	27,481,344	.
BRITISH COLUMBIA	LMb+	16,763,126	17,727,662	6,533,506	41,024,295	.
BROWN	Mb+	11,511,759	9,423,968	2,536,908	23,472,635	.
CALGARY	LM+	12,140,520	15,367,141	1,277,863	28,785,524	279,708
CALIFORNIA, BERKELEY	Lb+	22,726,792	26,980,912	12,951,485	62,659,189	1,104,629
CALIFORNIA, DAVIS	LMb+	8,940,658	9,160,816	1,602,610	19,704,084	956,318
CALIFORNIA, IRVINE	LMb+	9,318,324	10,135,792	1,550,253	21,004,369	896,806
CALIFORNIA, LOS ANGELES	LM+	15,610,465	27,728,222	9,427,546	52,766,233	1,211,590
CALIFORNIA, RIVERSIDE	+	4,424,542	5,845,948	2,111,241	12,381,731	673,221
CALIFORNIA, SAN DIEGO	M+	9,566,270	14,097,968	4,197,168	27,861,406	895,022
CALIFORNIA, SANTA BARBARA	+	5,860,806	8,436,162	3,287,609	17,584,577	711,296
CASE WESTERN RESERVE	LMb+	7,656,923	5,494,541	1,598,538	14,750,002	220,534
CHICAGO	LMb+	19,176,653	13,806,193	3,409,443	36,392,289	250,000
CINCINNATI	LMBb+	10,177,665	8,737,069	1,639,131	20,553,865	665,829
COLORADO	b+	11,200,366	9,244,867	1,643,291	22,088,524	21,319
COLORADO STATE	b+	7,823,526	7,434,683	1,488,479	16,746,688	363,658
COLUMBIA	LM+	29,500,049	31,607,063	5,325,286	66,432,398	.
CONNECTICUT	LMBb+	10,693,308	10,932,537	1,035,808	22,661,653	1,563,863
CORNELL	LMB+	21,560,997	23,986,642	6,195,913	51,743,552	.
DARTMOUTH	Mb+	10,695,121	9,062,060	1,889,546	21,646,727	.
DELAWARE	+	10,469,873	8,110,343	1,768,688	20,348,904	.
DUKE	LMb+	18,720,375	15,841,735	17,545,307	52,107,417	203,400
EMORY	LMB+	17,697,641	16,165,758	6,161,784	40,025,183	185,878

Overall Expenditures

	Notes	Total Library Materials 7	Total Salaries and Wages 8	Other Operating Expenditures 9	Total Library Expenditures 6	Bibl. Utilities, Networks, etc. External Expenditures 12
FLORIDA	LMBb+	12,827,981	13,643,423	4,736,497	31,207,901	538,347
FLORIDA STATE	LMBb+	9,440,934	7,855,731	634,803	17,931,468	135,132
GEORGE WASHINGTON	LMB+	12,193,022	11,887,219	3,143,363	27,223,604	.
GEORGETOWN	LMBb+	14,399,422	12,688,994	2,781,056	29,869,472	7,173
GEORGIA	Lb+	12,831,691	10,738,365	1,345,227	24,915,283	.
GEORGIA TECH	+	7,474,554	6,472,220	1,125,202	15,071,976	.
GUELPH	B+	7,160,715	7,307,099	977,447	15,445,261	.
HARVARD	LMb+	44,854,018	59,113,672	19,167,565	123,135,255	1,136,548
HAWAII	LMb+	7,856,488	9,968,725	1,147,083	18,972,296	642,210
HOUSTON	Lb+	11,419,248	7,586,149	2,092,779	21,098,176	.
HOWARD	LMb+	5,769,950	4,761,220	134,210	10,665,380	30,900
ILLINOIS, CHICAGO	Mb+	8,053,918	8,112,088	5,399,924	21,565,930	.
ILLINOIS, URBANA	Lb+	19,212,701	22,549,786	4,716,983	46,479,470	.
INDIANA	L+	16,027,788	14,801,772	3,658,049	34,487,609	229,540
IOWA	LM+	18,603,258	11,883,298	1,370,969	31,857,525	.
IOWA STATE	+	13,756,647	6,942,790	1,250,361	21,949,798	.
JOHNS HOPKINS	MB+	18,496,385	14,074,705	8,676,400	41,247,490	185,742
KANSAS	LMBb+	10,131,719	10,936,163	2,430,660	23,498,542	.
KENT STATE	+	5,381,081	4,725,057	709,690	10,815,828	760,827
KENTUCKY	LMb+	10,976,643	8,709,042	2,171,585	21,857,270	.
LAVAL	LM+	11,952,746	10,231,488	738,588	22,922,822	.
LOUISIANA STATE	LMb+	7,208,499	5,833,398	1,073,412	14,115,309	89,157
LOUISVILLE	MBb+	9,924,829	6,236,500	1,769,972	17,931,301	198,201
MCGILL	LMBb+	16,657,221	11,953,042	3,703,497	32,313,761	.
MCMASTER	Mb+	9,111,792	6,530,598	906,594	16,548,985	2,064
MANITOBA	LMb+	9,405,558	11,299,862	2,603,641	23,309,060	.
MARYLAND	b+	11,400,148	12,632,570	3,712,597	27,745,315	376,221
MASSACHUSETTS	+	7,571,461	8,584,426	2,054,907	18,210,794	75,000
MIT	b+	9,876,035	10,450,374	2,033,098	22,359,507	.
MIAMI	LMb+	13,280,160	10,285,400	2,397,729	25,963,289	.

OVERALL EXPENDITURES

	Notes	Total Library Materials 7	Total Salaries and Wages 8	Other Operating Expenditures 9	Total Library Expenditures 6	Bibl. Utilities, Networks, etc. External Expenditures 12
MICHIGAN	LM+	25,459,121	33,922,216	10,381,986	69,763,323	151,412
MICHIGAN STATE	L+	16,308,972	12,655,783	3,182,686	32,147,441	.
MINNESOTA	LMb+	17,963,662	18,653,609	4,735,995	41,353,266	563,082
MISSOURI	LM+	8,660,675	7,198,027	2,273,789	18,132,491	.
MONTREAL	LMb+	12,510,606	18,365,838	1,987,081	32,863,525	41,557
NEBRASKA	Lb+	8,618,714	7,318,148	1,958,039	17,894,901	126,000
NEW MEXICO	LMb+	9,341,631	9,533,839	3,783,040	22,658,510	2,338,325
NEW YORK	LMBb+	27,275,816	23,906,160	8,399,666	59,581,642	.
NORTH CAROLINA	LM+	15,557,364	18,731,906	3,731,461	38,020,731	44,552
NORTH CAROLINA STATE	+	10,679,211	13,469,704	7,730,527	31,879,442	.
NORTHWESTERN	LMBb+	15,702,473	15,265,127	3,346,325	34,313,925	.
NOTRE DAME	Lb+	13,352,304	11,183,546	2,238,097	26,773,947	.
OHIO	MBb+	4,993,681	5,064,842	1,371,906	11,430,429	723,400
OHIO STATE	LMb+	18,977,914	19,790,061	9,853,452	48,621,427	1,202,507
OKLAHOMA	LM+	14,299,029	7,881,309	3,091,723	25,272,061	.
OKLAHOMA STATE	MBb+	8,882,554	6,689,091	2,808,106	18,379,751	511,458
OREGON	LBb+	7,443,692	9,989,312	1,935,585	19,368,589	.
OTTAWA	LM+	13,959,115	9,598,213	2,316,610	25,873,938	.
PENNSYLVANIA	LM	18,385,481	20,621,052	6,501,490	45,508,023	460,549
PENNSYLVANIA STATE	LMBb+	20,287,723	26,558,591	7,902,069	54,748,383	21,250
PITTSBURGH	LMB+	16,617,295	12,105,408	3,225,860	31,948,563	529,543
PRINCETON	b+	25,837,011	20,752,134	4,683,216	51,272,361	.
PURDUE	+	13,428,913	8,982,400	4,085,003	26,496,316	340,162
QUEEN'S	LMb+	8,921,980	7,581,395	1,126,671	17,630,047	.
RICE	+	9,946,063	5,579,013	863,558	16,388,634	.
ROCHESTER	Mb+	9,944,292	8,111,516	3,412,424	21,468,232	182,880
RUTGERS	LBM+	14,110,365	23,916,544	2,874,076	40,900,985	.
SASKATCHEWAN	LM+	11,708,485	9,323,336	1,840,796	22,872,616	.
SOUTH CAROLINA	LMb+	8,941,910	8,654,362	6,487,475	24,083,747	.
SOUTHERN CALIFORNIA	LMBb+	22,428,916	18,763,146	3,944,160	45,136,222	10,444

OVERALL EXPENDITURES

	Notes	Total Library Materials 7	Total Salaries and Wages 8	Other Operating Expenditures 9	Total Library Expenditures 6	Bibl. Utilities, Networks, etc. External Expenditures 12
SOUTHERN ILLINOIS	LM+	6,948,240	5,292,410	655,901	12,896,551	52,011
SUNY-ALBANY	b+	6,033,091	5,913,708	430,984	12,377,783	160,633
SUNY-BUFFALO	LM+	9,065,327	9,490,524	1,405,801	19,961,652	38,389
SUNY-STONY BROOK	Mb+	8,401,621	4,831,659	457,931	13,691,211	35,164
SYRACUSE	Lb+	9,570,554	9,075,096	1,512,432	20,158,082	.
TEMPLE	LMBb+	11,511,310	8,692,742	2,339,353	22,543,405	.
TENNESSEE	LMBb+	14,781,177	10,219,802	1,291,992	26,292,971	10,207
TEXAS	L+	20,922,649	22,317,216	10,647,359	53,887,224	.
TEXAS A&M	MBLb+	23,609,080	14,276,051	4,057,764	41,942,895	4,086,798
TEXAS TECH	LMB+	14,256,641	11,810,949	3,104,400	29,171,990	54,750
TORONTO	LMB+	29,724,687	37,545,305	13,551,856	80,821,848	.
TULANE	LMB+	11,913,606	6,344,619	1,317,445	19,575,670	.
UTAH	LMb+	8,796,235	12,912,778	3,417,100	25,126,113	1,792,852
VANDERBILT	LM+	11,950,301	9,972,648	2,570,105	24,493,054	.
VIRGINIA	LMb+	12,109,120	17,053,495	4,997,620	34,160,235	933,249
VIRGINIA TECH	b+	9,161,016	7,140,129	2,178,622	18,479,767	1,250,117
WASHINGTON	LMBb+	16,067,994	20,841,881	5,690,848	42,600,723	442,042
WASHINGTON STATE	Bb+	6,847,684	6,205,117	721,711	13,774,512	36,341
WASHINGTON U.-ST. LOUIS	LMb+	13,711,438	10,208,127	3,102,065	27,021,630	2,845
WATERLOO	+	8,864,282	7,412,323	1,577,443	17,854,047	.
WAYNE STATE	LMb+	9,463,490	7,744,786	1,954,637	19,162,913	.
WESTERN	Lb+	13,289,824	9,000,822	1,970,950	24,261,596	.
WISCONSIN	LM+	12,797,066	20,868,378	5,698,427	39,363,871	1,523,946
YALE	LMb+	38,783,883	37,973,327	10,828,300	87,585,510	.
YORK	LB+	10,995,381	12,868,863	1,781,070	25,645,315	.
BOSTON PUBLIC	b+	4,463,585	24,181,779	9,565,068	38,210,432	.
NATL RES COUNCIL CANADA	b+	.	.	.	17,397,770	.
CENTER FOR RESEARCH LIBS	+	1,234,430	2,844,870	.	4,079,300	.
LIBRARY OF CONGRESS	LBb+	24,539,936	314,195,170	280,064,894	618,800,000	.
NATL AGRICULTURAL LIB	+	5,468,996	10,682,082	10,349,981	26,501,059	0

Overall Expenditures

	Notes	Total Library Materials 7	Total Salaries and Wages 8	Other Operating Expenditures 9	Total Library Expenditures 6	Bibl. Utilities, Networks, etc. External Expenditures 12
NATL ARCHIVES	+	106,000	182,478,826	203,215,174	385,800,000	0
NATL LIB OF MEDICINE	+	3,166,118	22,607,517	42,576,618	68,350,253	0
NEW YORK PUBLIC	+	12,752,000	47,244,000	29,763,000	89,759,000	.
NEW YORK STATE		2,139,711	4,387,180	1,066,754	7,593,645	37,050
SMITHSONIAN	+	2,211,929	7,818,252	3,268,353	13,298,534	59,783

+ - See Footnotes
L - Includes Law Library
M - Includes Medical Library

B - Includes branch campuses
b - Basis of volume count is bibliographic
. - Unavailable, not applicable or no data supplied

Overall Expenditures
Summary Data

		Total Library Materials 7	Total Salaries and Wages 8	Other Operating Expenditures 9	Total Library Expenditures 6	Bibl. Utilities, Networks, etc. External Expenditures 12
University Libraries	Mean	13,339,807	12,890,333	3,587,665	29,817,805	532,121
	Median	11,708,485	10,219,802	2,430,660	24,659,123	264,854
	High	44,854,018	59,113,672	19,167,565	123,135,255	4,086,798
	Low	4,424,542	4,709,273	134,210	10,665,380	2,064
	Totals	1,534,077,856	1,482,388,259	412,581,487	3,429,047,601	34,055,771
	Number of Libraries Reporting	115	115	115	115	64
Nonuniversity Libraries	Median	3,166,118	22,607,517	20,056,491	32,355,746	48,417
	Totals	56,082,705	616,439,676	579,869,842	1,269,789,993	96,833
	Number of Libraries Reporting	9	9	8	10	2
Grand Totals		1,590,160,561	2,098,827,935	992,451,329	4,698,837,595	34,152,604

Personnel and Public Services

	Notes	Professional Staff 13a	Support Staff 13b	Student Assistants 13c	Total Staff 13	Library Presentations to Groups 14	Participants in Group Presentations 15
ALABAMA	LMb+	86	68	43	197	909	19,167
ALBERTA	LM+	83	179	27	289	518	15,455
ARIZONA	LMb+	82	111	41	234	967	15,291
ARIZONA STATE	LB+	61	134	.	195	836	17,875
AUBURN	b+	47	33	25	105	631	12,707
BOSTON	LMb+	107	88	83	278	1,116	19,816
BOSTON COLLEGE	Lb+	73	66	46	185	680	12,202
BRIGHAM YOUNG	L+	113	58	196	367	2,786	52,855
BRITISH COLUMBIA	LMb+	135	145	47	327	1,464	35,638
BROWN	Mb+	72	77	30	179	318	6,785
CALGARY	LM+	69	152	21	242	719	16,261
CALIFORNIA, BERKELEY	Lb+	247	133	120	500	1,114	21,609
CALIFORNIA, DAVIS	LMb+	44	86	28	158	682	17,795
CALIFORNIA, IRVINE	LMb+	55	106	28	189	683	17,119
CALIFORNIA, LOS ANGELES	LM+	165	222	117	504	2,313	22,425
CALIFORNIA, RIVERSIDE	+	35	59	23	117	582	14,759
CALIFORNIA, SAN DIEGO	M+	111	108	52	271	308	9,654
CALIFORNIA, SANTA BARBARA	+	40	81	29	150	538	6,706
CASE WESTERN RESERVE	LMb+	58	32	27	117	772	10,309
CHICAGO	LMb+	72	180	52	304	665	11,471
CINCINNATI	LMBb+	92	43	42	177	1,428	28,537
COLORADO	b+	69	96	50	215	909	17,182
COLORADO STATE	b+	66	75	35	176	660	14,643
COLUMBIA	LM+	317	194	78	589	1,385	26,550
CONNECTICUT	LMBb+	83	59	68	210	1,202	23,431
CORNELL	LMB+	210	181	102	493	1,489	26,910
DARTMOUTH	Mb+	65	102	28	195	687	10,189
DELAWARE	+	60	77	23	160	539	12,806
DUKE	LMb+	189	101	27	317	1,223	16,714
EMORY	LMB+	136	155	57	348	976	15,629

Personnel and Public Services

	Notes	Reference Transactions 16	Initial Circulations 17	Full-text article requests 18	Regular Searches 19	Federated Searches 20	Total Items Loaned (ILL) 21	Total Items Borrowed (ILL) 22
ALABAMA	LMb+	50,684	98,205	2,401,854	67,122,805	0	16,603	10,176
ALBERTA	LM+	82,106	256,692	.	.	90,571,651	36,153	15,647
ARIZONA	LMb+	35,320	325,135	6,617,678	5,563,698	0	56,244	47,537
ARIZONA STATE	LB+	49,289	149,990	4,662,637	12,491,314	57,502	39,964	33,578
AUBURN	b+	ß 24,128	123,543	1,335,355	2,633,384	0	22,482	11,786
BOSTON	LMb+	35,834	92,756	3,414,071	6,081,451	44,851	17,189	12,001
BOSTON COLLEGE	Lb+	20,713	157,347	1,136,064	5,262,451	804,161	28,195	32,015
BRIGHAM YOUNG	L+	53,511	296,539	5,394,078	6,198,228	4,047,805	33,887	26,291
BRITISH COLUMBIA	LMb+	54,648	318,718	8,837,144	.	.	23,428	7,898
BROWN	Mb+	7,935	134,583	1,732,105	910,012	2,247	38,806	35,737
CALGARY	LM+	80,517	191,676	4,131,789	3,573,186	.	13,842	17,293
CALIFORNIA, BERKELEY	Lb+	57,546	371,653	.	.	.	27,009	16,850
CALIFORNIA, DAVIS	LMb+	46,227	119,142	15,211	33,515	148,377	27,040	16,848
CALIFORNIA, IRVINE	LMb+	30,340	102,761	.	.	.	16,263	20,305
CALIFORNIA, LOS ANGELES	LM+	102,818	486,211	8,095,130	6,584,789	645,139	35,703	34,424
CALIFORNIA, RIVERSIDE	+	14,456	76,937	2,539,227	540,898	0	13,711	11,660
CALIFORNIA, SAN DIEGO	M+	51,692	196,155	0	3,586,011	0	18,270	15,985
CALIFORNIA, SANTA BARBARA	+	40,333	120,629	2,092,759	.	.	14,016	35,782
CASE WESTERN RESERVE	LMb+	6,560	64,320	2,770,187	2,267,474	0	33,507	22,836
CHICAGO	LMb+	18,017	234,328	9,083,092	35,406,014	2,340,410	63,077	41,390
CINCINNATI	LMBb+	ß 42,709	143,463	2,062,788	4,810,645	0	45,656	28,504
COLORADO	b+	35,843	231,003	2,235,901	3,252,595	12,946,858	82,629	34,502
COLORADO STATE	b+	ß 56,192	108,667	2,292,357	2,255,986	25,822	82,192	60,515
COLUMBIA	LM+	65,735	315,580	11,939,338	55,852,563	790,517	54,391	48,833
CONNECTICUT	LMBb+	18,004	112,258	5,264,048	5,418,899	833,951	44,074	57,961
CORNELL	LMB+	51,627	245,065	4,943,178	.	.	51,716	49,841
DARTMOUTH	Mb+	9,742	208,475	1,342,417	8,211,682	258,118	50,003	31,652
DELAWARE	+	ß 143,971	244,117	.	1,713,776	475,125	23,377	15,645
DUKE	LMb+	33,142	387,067	.	.	.	34,795	35,942
EMORY	LMB+	20,568	203,038	797,306	559,106	105,553	28,962	11,513

Personnel and Public Services

	Notes	Professional Staff 13a	Support Staff 13b	Student Assistants 13c	Total Staff 13	Library Presentations to Groups 14	Participants in Group Presentations 15
FLORIDA	LMBb+	87	177	48	312	1,051	21,466
FLORIDA STATE	LMBb+	88	72	99	259	1,050	19,710
GEORGE WASHINGTON	LMB+	67	96	58	221	2,514	31,524
GEORGETOWN	LMBb+	100	94	44	238	2,686	23,118
GEORGIA	Lb+	79	164	50	293	1,116	17,544
GEORGIA TECH	+	52	79	5	136	391	7,497
GUELPH	B+	54	60	10	124	2,348	46,300
HARVARD	LMb+	464	330	.	794	1,710	23,605
HAWAII	LMb+	80	71	55	206	590	9,566
HOUSTON	Lb+	72	66	40	178	713	12,397
HOWARD	LMb+	37	51	30	118	463	10,213
ILLINOIS, CHICAGO	Mb+	75	76	31	182	791	11,146
ILLINOIS, URBANA	Lb+	167	168	100	435	1,724	27,807
INDIANA	L+	152	137	108	397	1,313	22,694
IOWA	LM+	108	86	49	243	1,185	19,098
IOWA STATE	+	39	81	23	143	452	14,666
JOHNS HOPKINS	MB+	124	109	36	269	1,196	12,180
KANSAS	LMBb+	70	124	59	253	1,067	15,614
KENT STATE	+	52	18	38	108	461	9,715
KENTUCKY	LMb+	93	80	45	218	910	17,422
LAVAL	LM+	66	148	0	214	399	12,134
LOUISIANA STATE	LMb+	57	64	31	152	982	24,345
LOUISVILLE	MBb+	55	60	30	145	1,037	22,936
MCGILL	LMBb+	92	84	14	190	873	20,126
MCMASTER	Mb+	49	70	14	133	320	11,722
MANITOBA	LMb+	60	115	18	193	ß 1,225	ß 13,139
MARYLAND	b+	138	83	53	274	935	18,982
MASSACHUSETTS	+	59	64	38	161	391	8,851
MIT	b+	91	71	15	177	419	9,475
MIAMI	LMb+	88	106	62	256	853	19,014

Personnel and Public Services

	Notes	Reference Transactions 16	Initial Circulations 17	Full-text article requests 18	Regular Searches 19	Federated Searches 20	Total Items Loaned (ILL) 21	Total Items Borrowed (ILL) 22
FLORIDA	LMBb+	34,252	273,624	3,580,044	3,971,591	.	26,081	21,873
FLORIDA STATE	LMBb+	ß 79,187	154,234	2,158,314	3,178,285	68,219	21,490	11,920
GEORGE WASHINGTON	LMB+	29,535	125,377	3,053,361	4,319,145	100,139	24,801	50,767
GEORGETOWN	LMBb+	ß 58,873	184,655	3,127,386	2,339,426	67,369	45,344	29,411
GEORGIA	Lb+	37,196	201,148	3,018,281	9,330,867	1,283,576	38,641	8,807
GEORGIA TECH	+	11,435	89,346	.	.	.	11,546	10,989
GUELPH	B+	8,056	81,938	1,455,267	.	.	21,905	15,533
HARVARD	LMb+	114,618	650,514	.	.	.	52,485	39,043
HAWAII	LMb+	23,199	113,962	1,836,896	4,381,346	45,605	5,037	20,918
HOUSTON	Lb+	33,216	111,344	694,879	3,919,933	1,396,406	25,669	17,049
HOWARD	LMb+	41,941	27,989	123,230	1,297,807	0	6,961	2,513
ILLINOIS, CHICAGO	Mb+	29,215	78,451	2,882,711	3,297,199	22,700	45,406	42,798
ILLINOIS, URBANA	Lb+	ß 107,251	446,722	5,216,733	48,206,156	.	86,226	66,825
INDIANA	L+	ß 29,494	414,722	.	.	.	34,470	36,244
IOWA	LM+	ß 53,709	141,896	2,273,586	4,759,580	1,702,832	43,751	21,391
IOWA STATE	+	12,992	99,759	739,049	1,480,165	1,540,171	27,138	8,908
JOHNS HOPKINS	MB+	28,583	166,072	6,065,343	3,519,964	0	40,480	30,050
KANSAS	LMBb+	32,201	195,974	1,917,098	1,546,462	40,683	36,905	20,668
KENT STATE	+	26,382	206,814	286,010	4,353,504	.	7,475	9,130
KENTUCKY	LMb+	22,681	114,181	2,806,040	3,754,353	0	25,262	18,390
LAVAL	LM+	32,525	268,292	2,872,400	2,979,563	0	18,144	6,310
LOUISIANA STATE	LMb+	ß 18,110	58,727	1,398,275	4,943,144	80,951,747	16,472	14,252
LOUISVILLE	MBb+	33,727	112,698	1,022,434	611,970	485,735	18,196	16,990
MCGILL	LMBb+	ß 54,175	263,902	.	.	.	10,556	12,547
MCMASTER	Mb+	10,060	109,815	2,804,712	.	.	9,181	9,088
MANITOBA	LMb+	ß 87,337	132,492	2,386,847	2,153,161	0	11,386	18,347
MARYLAND	b+	19,392	147,441	4,846,367	13,157,249	117,831	20,651	35,146
MASSACHUSETTS	+	30,086	107,226	1,602,176	3,656,736	0	28,634	38,673
MIT	b+	ß 18,875	118,987	5,570,657	41,554,405	63,562	27,836	15,935
MIAMI	LMb+	37,197	124,473	1,730,555	619,687	703,631	27,607	10,648

Personnel and Public Services

	Notes	Professional Staff 13a	Support Staff 13b	Student Assistants 13c	Total Staff 13	Library Presentations to Groups 14	Participants in Group Presentations 15
MICHIGAN	LM+	204	340	125	669	1,462	30,918
MICHIGAN STATE	L+	86	111	67	264	923	37,458
MINNESOTA	LMb+	117	177	69	363	1,096	21,535
MISSOURI	LM+	52	104	30	186	904	14,278
MONTREAL	LMb+	115	222	3	340	1,398	25,821
NEBRASKA	Lb+	44	96	36	176	329	7,198
NEW MEXICO	LMb+	54	116	51	221	1,549	18,744
NEW YORK	LMBb+	255	153	77	485	1,584	24,609
NORTH CAROLINA	LM+	125	169	79	373	1,491	33,374
NORTH CAROLINA STATE	+	127	79	52	258	749	20,260
NORTHWESTERN	LMBb+	140	134	87	361	762	10,289
NOTRE DAME	Lb+	104	99	27	230	467	8,695
OHIO	MBb+	44	45	30	119	416	8,284
OHIO STATE	LMb+	151	162	373	686	1,244	41,729
OKLAHOMA	LM+	67	88	74	229	1,530	17,954
OKLAHOMA STATE	MBb+	61	65	66	192	817	16,370
OREGON	LBb+	86	80	61	227	875	22,649
OTTAWA	LM+	48	103	8	159	595	13,933
PENNSYLVANIA	LM	148	182	108	438	1,705	23,633
PENNSYLVANIA STATE	LMBb+	210	368	55	633	2,875	92,156
PITTSBURGH	LMB+	110	137	55	302	1,122	18,444
PRINCETON	b+	148	171	50	369	.	.
PURDUE	+	81	78	48	207	551	13,933
QUEEN'S	LMb+	39	76	16	131	830	14,709
RICE	+	63	48	9	120	290	3,486
ROCHESTER	Mb+	87	56	45	188	890	14,178
RUTGERS	LBM+	109	243	93	445	2,112	28,258
SASKATCHEWAN	LM+	58	75	14	147	582	15,476
SOUTH CAROLINA	LMb+	74	89	99	262	2,242	14,814
SOUTHERN CALIFORNIA	LMBb+	134	134	88	356	1,436	41,249

Personnel and Public Services

	Notes	Reference Transactions 16	Initial Circulations 17	Full-text article requests 18	Regular Searches 19	Federated Searches 20	Total Items Loaned (ILL) 21	Total Items Borrowed (ILL) 22
MICHIGAN	LM+	102,143	437,026	8,270,897	13,807,584	5,200	58,462	56,229
MICHIGAN STATE	L+	47,230	341,021	3,926,184	4,532,658	.	69,225	21,065
MINNESOTA	LMb+	30,516	229,314	.	.	4,598,474	131,918	31,187
MISSOURI	LM+	35,096	145,570	2,547,164	3,518,330	.	47,875	36,205
MONTREAL	LMb+	72,098	373,600	5,174,917	8,140,668	432,642	15,104	17,382
NEBRASKA	Lb+	ß 27,519	157,739	1,220,843	40,638,408	0	26,909	25,011
NEW MEXICO	LMb+	21,293	245,237	2,725,953	5,863,373	760,504	27,835	36,678
NEW YORK	LMBb+	129,253	297,543	7,773,372	6,854,605	738,444	21,922	31,975
NORTH CAROLINA	LM+	83,458	440,955	3,225,221	6,058,905	829,162	51,217	24,454
NORTH CAROLINA STATE	+	ß 37,428	132,105	3,368,505	4,139,299	1,498,538	14,854	28,722
NORTHWESTERN	LMBb+	19,836	154,374	4,100,819	1,432,478	82,081	39,687	44,740
NOTRE DAME	Lb+	23,680	159,736	.	.	.	28,832	27,739
OHIO	MBb+	13,840	155,181	1,608,589	2,434,932	228,665	42,807	39,703
OHIO STATE	LMb+	21,524	384,857	5,070,881	9,304,375	55,592	106,507	95,791
OKLAHOMA	LM+	51,046	128,186	2,253,085	16,162,911	6,828,298	57,782	31,697
OKLAHOMA STATE	MBb+	48,825	232,721	2,420,506	6,549,499	811,083	33,753	17,394
OREGON	LBb+	ß 38,963	140,724	2,060,085	6,466,874	1,163,874	66,526	59,165
OTTAWA	LM+	40,620	219,576	2,115,686	885,731	.	14,584	7,998
PENNSYLVANIA	LM	.	258,190	6,249,915	3,724,712	.	79,297	106,494
PENNSYLVANIA STATE	LMBb+	ß 74,155	385,129	4,019,888	.	.	71,572	43,452
PITTSBURGH	LMB+	60,899	170,594	9,222,912	8,403,027	.	49,343	21,474
PRINCETON	b+	.	231,482	688,695	.	.	48,459	40,709
PURDUE	+	28,232	79,998	4,221,040	5,980,815	984,036	27,306	25,508
QUEEN'S	LMb+	13,933	120,918	1,828,407	.	2,072,368	9,429	4,496
RICE	+	.	110,268	.	.	.	16,289	11,571
ROCHESTER	Mb+	ß 24,153	138,743	1,822,869	989,506	0	16,382	20,381
RUTGERS	LBM+	50,450	199,206	2,085,813	6,647,442	2,401,967	55,109	57,131
SASKATCHEWAN	LM+	14,238	101,987	1,929,409	.	.	5,537	4,980
SOUTH CAROLINA	LMb+	63,169	133,342	1,502,333	22,073,689	295,061	16,549	18,936
SOUTHERN CALIFORNIA	LMBb+	87,698	153,002	3,883,683	46,814,707	230,822	32,994	20,164

PERSONNEL AND PUBLIC SERVICES

	Notes	Professional Staff 13a	Support Staff 13b	Student Assistants 13c	Total Staff 13	Library Presentations to Groups 14	Participants in Group Presentations 15
SOUTHERN ILLINOIS	LM+	42	61	33	136	1,181	12,127
SUNY-ALBANY	b+	63	33	27	123	467	6,715
SUNY-BUFFALO	LM+	94	40	40	174	693	18,445
SUNY-STONY BROOK	Mb+	63	13	29	105	332	7,789
SYRACUSE	Lb+	82	100	18	200	585	9,970
TEMPLE	LMBb+	74	70	47	191	1,189	30,067
TENNESSEE	LMBb+	98	116	31	245	947	19,942
TEXAS	L+	148	226	112	486	1,274	24,740
TEXAS A&M	MBLb+	149	125	66	340	1,071	42,706
TEXAS TECH	LMB+	103	146	71	320	2,252	16,010
TORONTO	LMB+	192	322	133	647	1,799	40,795
TULANE	LMB+	52	80	30	162	559	13,046
UTAH	LMb+	84	164	77	325	ß 1,789	ß 40,306
VANDERBILT	LM+	87	88	23	198	713	14,278
VIRGINIA	LMb+	136	160	46	342	1,742	21,041
VIRGINIA TECH	b+	66	76	40	182	794	15,926
WASHINGTON	LMBb+	181	161	90	432	1,511	40,560
WASHINGTON STATE	Bb+	45	70	26	141	1,308	41,748
WASHINGTON U.-ST. LOUIS	LMb+	103	95	38	236	918	11,375
WATERLOO	+	37	86	31	154	191	8,881
WAYNE STATE	LMb+	97	40	70	207	322	6,604
WESTERN	Lb+	71	90	11	172	507	14,211
WISCONSIN	LM+	231	128	186	545	1,790	32,272
YALE	LMb+	243	283	51	577	1,360	22,588
YORK	LB+	69	103	28	200	764	26,533
BOSTON PUBLIC	b+	184	191	24	399	10,239	186,289
NATL RES COUNCIL CANADA	b+	66	47	0	113	.	.
CENTER FOR RESEARCH LIBS	+	31	16	11	58	.	.
LIBRARY OF CONGRESS	LBb+	.	.	.	3,138	7,370	224,523
NATL AGRICULTURAL LIB	+	75	25	0	100	ß 72	ß 2,141

	Notes	Reference Transactions 16	Initial Circulations 17	Full-text article requests 18	Regular Searches 19	Federated Searches 20	Total Items Loaned (ILL) 21	Total Items Borrowed (ILL) 22
SOUTHERN ILLINOIS	LM+	62,871	144,310	779,114	725,049	.	50,318	35,743
SUNY-ALBANY	b+	40,020	47,082	901,440	3,128,118	14,310,603	15,599	26,156
SUNY-BUFFALO	LM+	ß 26,020	135,992	2,752,324	5,011,372	34,037	27,571	31,233
SUNY-STONY BROOK	Mb+	13,710	64,735	.	.	.	18,568	8,208
SYRACUSE	Lb+	27,883	87,934	933,324	1,666,707	12,426	27,511	17,549
TEMPLE	LMBb+	58,480	160,962	2,807,911	8,533,994	.	26,090	22,504
TENNESSEE	LMBb+	ß 48,710	173,605	3,060,434	4,678,951	723,339	28,708	15,876
TEXAS	L+	ß 88,713	324,486	4,819,233	2,494,795	2,815,867	40,881	25,099
TEXAS A&M	MBLb+	65,401	853,173	4,233,362	65,648,787	411,419	45,046	51,878
TEXAS TECH	LMB+	87,468	132,994	3,773,685	22,957,059	701,613	37,271	34,527
TORONTO	LMB+	205,770	755,382	.	.	.	32,496	9,457
TULANE	LMB+	16,078	95,187	1,487,058	6,078,233	1,146,140	13,497	10,431
UTAH	LMb+	ß 139,211	143,036	2,653,649	3,793,436	.	32,840	23,377
VANDERBILT	LM+	15,628	148,916	2,718,430	21,602,627	2,615	21,965	20,690
VIRGINIA	LMb+	ß 64,891	243,069	2,648,037	3,399,190	.	29,359	32,421
VIRGINIA TECH	b+	12,499	119,613	2,514,282	5,472,480	.	14,686	30,753
WASHINGTON	LMBb+	ß 49,929	410,804	5,613,975	10,000,000	.	38,111	75,889
WASHINGTON STATE	Bb+	ß 16,393	102,767	1,907,149	38,621,567	192,053	.	32,266
WASHINGTON U.-ST. LOUIS	LMb+	ß 69,740	136,585	4,675,659	3,075,490	231,079	46,423	41,675
WATERLOO	+	14,180	92,922	2,597,736	2,921,979	17,557	20,159	23,644
WAYNE STATE	LMb+	22,255	34,160	2,819,624	1,253,149	2,527,284	25,048	31,054
WESTERN	Lb+	21,277	211,695	.	.	.	11,176	9,660
WISCONSIN	LM+	ß 12,310	360,243	7,464,468	23,411,005	1,281,603	125,502	81,149
YALE	LMb+	ß 41,791	379,984	8,535,826	41,558,313	433,128	74,958	87,135
YORK	LB+	32,079	308,526	3,469,115	21,373,886	.	9,470	4,739
BOSTON PUBLIC	b+	398,596	3,722,705	.	.	.	26,756	6,282
NATL RES COUNCIL CANADA	b+	.	.	.	.	.	.	.
CENTER FOR RESEARCH LIBS	+	.	.	.	.	.	.	.
LIBRARY OF CONGRESS	LBb+	467,142	982,052	.	.	78,100,000	25,432	.
NATL AGRICULTURAL LIB	+	8,066	1,515	1,273,446	361,125	0	5,169	2,058

Personnel and Public Services

	Notes	Professional Staff 13a	Support Staff 13b	Student Assistants 13c	Total Staff 13	Library Presentations to Groups 14	Participants in Group Presentations 15
NATL ARCHIVES	+	423	2,078	154	2,655	1,235	53,694
NATL LIB OF MEDICINE	+	199	47	8	254	134	5,411
NEW YORK PUBLIC	+	163	206	63	432	1,501	70,192
NEW YORK STATE		30	48	13	91	30	1,182
SMITHSONIAN	+	81	36	0	117	781	7,376

+ - See Footnotes
L - Includes Law Library
M - Includes Medical Library
B - Includes branch campuses

b - Basis of volume count is bibliographic
. - Unavailable, not applicable or no data supplied
β - Figure derived from a sampling method rather than an actual count

Personnel and Public Services

	Notes	Reference Transactions 16	Initial Circulations 17	Full-text article requests 18	Regular Searches 19	Federated Searches 20	Total Items Loaned (ILL) 21	Total Items Borrowed (ILL) 22
NATL ARCHIVES	+	3,379	144	2,000	0	0	5	50
NATL LIB OF MEDICINE	+	118,158	70,119	.	.	.	155,615	77
NEW YORK PUBLIC	+	466,578	.	513,409	6,809,801	.	7,691	8,351
NEW YORK STATE		57,061	11,652	129,155	485,197	0	38,415	2,890
SMITHSONIAN	+	21,968	24,701	60,869	136,778	76,395	2,478	4,733

+ - See Footnotes
L - Includes Law Library
M - Includes Medical Library
B - Includes branch campuses

b - Basis of volume count is bibliographic
. - Unavailable, not applicable or no data supplied
β - Figure derived from a sampling method rather than an actual count

Personnel and Public Services
Summary Data

		Professional Staff 13a	Support Staff 13b	Student Assistants 13c	Total Staff 13	Library Presentations to Groups 14	Participants in Group Presentations 15
University Libraries	Mean	101	114	54	268	1,045	19,961
	Median	83	96	45	221	914	17,302
	High	464	368	373	794	2,875	92,156
	Low	35	13	0	105	191	3,486
	Totals	11,608	13,081	6,097	30,786	119,148	2,275,605
	Number of Libraries Reporting	115	115	113	115	114	114
Nonuniversity Libraries	Median	81	47	11	186	1,008	30,535
	Totals	1,252	2,694	273	7,357	21,362	550,808
	Number of Libraries Reporting	9	9	9	10	8	8
Grand Totals		12,860	15,775	6,370	38,143	140,510	2,826,413

PERSONNEL AND PUBLIC SERVICES
Summary Data

		Reference Transactions 16	Initial Circulations 17	Full-text article requests 18	Regular Searches 19	Federated Searches 20	Total Items Loaned (ILL) 21	Total Items Borrowed (ILL) 22
University Libraries	Mean	44,735	204,916	3,290,879	10,244,488	3,184,125	34,967	28,640
	Median	35,577	154,374	2,722,192	4,605,805	231,079	28,415	24,454
	High	205,770	853,173	11,939,338	67,122,805	90,571,651	131,918	106,494
	Low	6,560	27,989	0	33,515	0	5,037	2,513
	Totals	5,010,309	23,565,314	329,087,871	942,492,895	251,545,867	3,986,238	3,293,654
	Number of Libraries Reporting	112	115	100	92	79	114	115
Nonuniversity Libraries	Median	87,610	24,701	129,155	361,125	0	16,562	2,890
	Totals	1,540,948	4,812,888	1,978,879	7,792,901	78,176,395	261,561	24,441
	Number of Libraries Reporting	8	7	5	5	5	8	7
Grand Totals		6,551,257	28,378,202	331,066,750	950,285,796	329,722,262	4,247,799	3,318,095

ANALYSIS OF SELECTED VARIABLES OF UNIVERSITY LIBRARIES, 2013–2014

The percentages and ratios below are select indicators that describe the condition of ARL university libraries. The high and low figures indicate the range, while the mean and median indicate the central tendency of the distributions for ARL university libraries. Note that a distribution is normal when the mean and the median figures are identical. If the mean is larger than the median, then the distribution is positively skewed, and if the opposite is true, the distribution is negatively skewed.

Category	High	Mean	Median	Low	Number of Libraries Reporting
Professional Staff as a precent of Total Staff	60.00	37.69	37.64	22.01	115
Support Staff as a precent of Total Staff	69.16	42.86	43.02	12.38	115
Student Assistant Staff as a precent of Total Staff	54.37	19.97	20.16	0.88	112
Ratio of Professional to Support Staff (excluding Student Assistant Staff)	4.85	1.01	0.88	0.40	115
Ratio of Items Loaned to Items Borrowed	4.39	1.41	1.19	0.24	114
Total Library Materials Expenditures as a precent of Total Library Expenditures	62.67	46.43	47.76	29.58	115
Salary and Wages Expenditures as a precent of Total Library Expenditures	58.47	42.69	42.48	30.40	115
Other Operating Expenditures as a precent of Total Library Expenditures	33.67	10.88	9.94	1.26	115
Library Expenditures per Faculty	74,088.60	18,151.28	16,458.28	6,857.90	115
Library Expenditures per Full-Time Student	7,343.47	1,327.02	994.52	353.46	115
Library Expenditures per Full-Time Graduate Student	19,053.27	5,225.33	4,634.52	2,441.64	115
Library Expenditures per Full-Time User	6,065.48	1,216.96	918.55	338.83	115
Library Expenditures per User	5,989.98	1,064.57	751.13	246.75	115
Library Expenditures per PhD Awarded	502,399.20	60,550.63	49,572.14	15,889.97	115
Library Staff per PhD Awarded	4.53	0.55	0.43	0.16	115
Professional Library Staff per PhD Awarded	1.73	0.20	0.17	0.04	115

FACULTY AND ENROLLMENT

	Notes	Doctor's Degrees Awarded 23	Doctor's Degree Fields 24	Faculty 25	Total Students (Full-time) 26	Total Students (Part-time) 27	Graduate Students (Full-time) 28	Graudate Students (Part-time) 29
ALABAMA	LMb+	329	49	1,130	29,036	5,258	2,488	2,363
ALBERTA	LM+	464	.	1,691	35,789	3,514	6,137	1,527
ARIZONA	LMb+	450	94	1,637	36,510	5,726	7,085	2,164
ARIZONA STATE	LB+	796	84	2,692	61,923	14,848	9,634	5,048
AUBURN	b+	490	63	1,184	21,093	3,771	3,082	1,983
BOSTON	LMb+	1,107	134	2,478	25,797	6,614	9,204	5,024
BOSTON COLLEGE	Lb+	444	25	758	12,921	1,388	3,502	1,039
BRIGHAM YOUNG	L+	100	24	1,237	25,084	2,681	2,030	1,328
BRITISH COLUMBIA	LMb+	540	87	2,764	42,387	15,897	9,122	1,430
BROWN	Mb+	227	46	871	8,527	416	2,359	129
CALGARY	LM+	324	52	1,749	28,944	2,551	5,272	599
CALIFORNIA, BERKELEY	Lb+	1,264	97	1,620	34,405	1,494	9,387	738
CALIFORNIA, DAVIS	LMb+	901	74	1,596	32,766	541	6,461	183
CALIFORNIA, IRVINE	LMb+	603	52	1,129	27,925	970	4,808	557
CALIFORNIA, LOS ANGELES	LM+	784	80	2,007	41,252	941	13,165	351
CALIFORNIA, RIVERSIDE	+	264	52	822	20,771	448	2,566	32
CALIFORNIA, SAN DIEGO	M+	624	63	1,309	27,401	1,050	4,548	141
CALIFORNIA, SANTA BARBARA	+	360	47	969	19,076	286	2,863	7
CASE WESTERN RESERVE	LMb+	655	58	667	9,270	1,055	4,742	922
CHICAGO	LMb+	711	70	1,964	12,960	2,228	7,309	2,143
CINCINNATI	LMBb+	768	104	1,157	25,873	8,506	5,541	5,132
COLORADO	b+	566	55	1,424	26,242	5,775	2,294	3,627
COLORADO STATE	b+	369	46	1,435	23,546	7,710	2,769	4,689
COLUMBIA	LM+	616	107	2,276	26,889	7,762	17,052	7,140
CONNECTICUT	LMBb+	800	61	1,877	25,874	4,589	5,339	2,709
CORNELL	LMB+	959	111	3,091	22,543	93	8,163	80
DARTMOUTH	Mb+	167	17	836	6,185	157	1,985	81
DELAWARE	+	244	58	1,174	19,685	2,481	2,833	846
DUKE	LMb+	1,100	53	1,136	14,894	571	8,265	554
EMORY	LMB+	270	41	2,300	13,181	1,332	5,505	1,172

Faculty and Enrollment

	Notes	Doctor's Degrees Awarded 23	Doctor's Degree Fields 24	Faculty 25	Total Students (Full-time) 26	Total Students (Part-time) 27	Graduate Students (Full-time) 28	Graduate Students (Part-time) 29
FLORIDA	LMBb+	1,964	90	3,468	42,490	7,388	12,176	4,590
FLORIDA STATE	LMBb+	802	439	1,494	35,658	6,340	5,943	2,100
GEORGE WASHINGTON	LMB+	1,091	53	1,343	18,650	8,643	9,041	7,895
GEORGETOWN	LMBb+	973	27	1,003	14,407	3,442	7,107	3,106
GEORGIA	Lb+	463	94	1,774	35,197	3,408	6,746	1,808
GEORGIA TECH	+	30	488	1,065	18,743	2,728	5,452	1,461
GUELPH	B+	136	.	760	20,273	2,114	2,120	225
HARVARD	LMb+	1,535	132	1,662	20,350	7,903	13,385	4,617
HAWAII	LMb+	366	70	1,435	15,548	5,675	3,401	2,903
HOUSTON	Lb+	314	41	1,388	28,488	11,052	5,983	3,157
HOWARD	LMb+	500	38	1,034	8,190	2,625	2,369	1,115
ILLINOIS, CHICAGO	Mb+	969	66	1,246	23,096	4,493	3,785	3,235
ILLINOIS, URBANA	Lb+	1,118	94	2,176	41,118	3,824	9,602	2,645
INDIANA	L+	771	91	2,014	37,467	9,350	6,417	3,538
IOWA	LM+	361	69	1,377	24,295	5,453	4,773	3,001
IOWA STATE	+	347	81	1,445	29,410	3,545	3,232	2,064
JOHNS HOPKINS	MB+	619	68	1,220	13,660	7,667	7,135	7,425
KANSAS	LMBb+	767	94	2,171	23,411	3,953	6,218	1,929
KENT STATE	+	147	49	1,321	30,600	11,913	3,323	2,910
KENTUCKY	LMb+	864	78	1,351	25,658	2,777	5,774	1,220
LAVAL	LM+	300	74	1,475	29,670	12,293	6,981	3,787
LOUISIANA STATE	LMb+	567	52	1,312	27,632	3,314	4,821	1,194
LOUISVILLE	MBb+	515	35	1,774	17,198	5,331	3,941	1,549
MANITOBA	LMb+	115	52	1,203	23,206	5,370	2,843	737
MARYLAND	b+	649	83	3,378	32,199	5,073	7,677	2,937
MASSACHUSETTS	+	303	47	1,263	22,808	5,710	2,303	4,081
MCGILL	LMBb+	857	97	3,108	32,071	6,222	9,293	2,275
MCMASTER	Mb+	245	43	1,413	29,765	3,990	4,264	856
MIAMI	LMb+	815	57	1,061	15,597	1,338	4,960	595
MICHIGAN	LM+	1,636	130	4,254	41,152	2,558	13,836	1,591

Faculty and Enrollment

	Notes	Doctor's Degrees Awarded 23	Doctor's Degree Fields 24	Faculty 25	Total Students (Full-time) 26	Total Students (Part-time) 27	Graduate Students (Full-time) 28	Graudate Students (Part-time) 29
MICHIGAN STATE	L+	1,510	114	2,770	44,007	6,206	9,169	3,059
MINNESOTA	LMb+	1,796	119	1,956	38,767	12,759	9,827	7,250
MISSOURI	LM+	877	73	1,409	30,670	4,314	5,068	2,634
MIT	b+	594	35	1,000	11,138	163	6,639	134
MONTREAL	LMb+	484	77	1,937	48,158	19,695	12,528	5,065
NEBRASKA	Lb+	436	44	1,310	20,873	3,552	2,771	2,278
NEW MEXICO	LMb+	678	40	3,304	21,065	8,051	5,876	2,507
NEW YORK	LMBb+	1,066	98	3,971	34,238	9,411	12,084	8,229
NORTH CAROLINA	LM+	538	61	1,630	24,390	4,737	6,820	3,937
NORTH CAROLINA STATE	+	575	63	1,783	26,770	7,239	5,301	4,712
NORTHWESTERN	LMBb+	492	67	3,256	15,458	4,001	6,999	3,440
NOTRE DAME	Lb+	386	43	1,118	11,908	216	3,449	198
OHIO	MBb+	273	93	1,100	24,208	14,649	2,693	2,589
OHIO STATE	LMb+	1,604	119	2,848	56,040	8,828	10,024	3,629
OKLAHOMA	LM+	992	95	2,376	24,236	6,522	5,453	3,463
OKLAHOMA STATE	MBb+	244	42	1,334	24,748	12,501	2,614	3,285
OREGON	LBb+	339	45	1,313	21,920	2,553	3,028	648
OTTAWA	LM+	239	50	1,269	35,159	7,428	5,237	1,308
PENNSYLVANIA	LM	1,244	72	1,978	21,344	3,286	11,025	2,080
PENNSYLVANIA STATE	LMBb+	986	114	5,927	73,567	18,852	7,311	7,616
PITTSBURGH	LMB+	1,086	99	1,889	31,044	3,970	7,586	2,448
PRINCETON	b+	389	72	904	8,014	0	2,691	0
PURDUE	+	958	64	2,063	34,871	4,923	6,212	3,136
QUEEN'S	LMb+	234	37	777	21,509	3,268	3,798	450
RICE	+	191	30	656	6,356	272	2,452	211
ROCHESTER	Mb+	380	62	2,028	9,284	1,736	3,447	1,396
RUTGERS	LBM+	1,951	93	3,322	52,612	12,849	11,141	8,414
SASKATCHEWAN	LM+	416	44	1,106	18,785	2,258	2,707	408
SOUTH CAROLINA	LMb+	834	69	1,816	28,655	3,942	6,122	2,295
SOUTHERN CALIFORNIA	LMBb+	663	89	1,883	35,775	5,239	18,486	4,529

FACULTY AND ENROLLMENT

	Notes	Doctor's Degrees Awarded 23	Doctor's Degree Fields 24	Faculty 25	Total Students (Full-time) 26	Total Students (Part-time) 27	Graduate Students (Full-time) 28	Graudate Students (Part-time) 29
SOUTHERN ILLINOIS	LM+	345	34	843	14,478	3,486	2,675	1,983
SUNY-ALBANY	b+	208	38	606	14,393	2,947	2,344	2,177
SUNY-BUFFALO	LM+	992	94	1,220	24,813	5,037	6,722	3,297
SUNY-STONY BROOK	Mb+	576	48	1,332	20,043	4,100	5,151	3,000
SYRACUSE	Lb+	169	53	1,049	19,092	2,175	4,670	1,500
TEMPLE	LMBb+	1,201	59	2,034	31,535	6,084	6,529	2,673
TENNESSEE	LMBb+	462	59	1,734	26,283	3,747	6,484	2,364
TEXAS	L+	1,355	91	2,446	47,416	4,643	10,517	1,563
TEXAS A&M	MBLb+	837	100	3,527	54,291	3,924	11,724	1,261
TEXAS TECH	LMB+	544	58	2,361	31,832	5,798	6,299	2,941
TORONTO	LMB+	879	96	2,407	72,201	7,681	14,381	1,503
TULANE	LMB+	981	41	1,059	13,867	2,559	6,775	812
UTAH	LMb+	836	74	1,428	23,438	8,993	6,119	1,820
VANDERBILT	LM+	671	58	3,353	11,965	792	5,201	721
VIRGINIA	LMb+	919	55	1,326	21,086	2,378	5,997	1,380
VIRGINIA TECH	b+	590	53	1,442	28,591	2,780	5,079	2,258
WASHINGTON	LMBb+	1,402	94	3,897	45,489	7,119	11,893	3,282
WASHINGTON STATE	Bb+	268	48	1,242	23,604	4,038	3,292	1,280
WASHINGTON U.-ST. LOUIS	LMb+	261	42	1,914	12,078	1,954	5,491	1,205
WATERLOO	+	347	61	1,139	33,140	2,792	4,035	1,265
WAYNE STATE	LMb+	807	56	1,041	18,096	9,801	5,875	3,420
WESTERN	Lb+	311	50	1,410	27,533	2,695	5,007	585
WISCONSIN	LM+	813	104	3,297	38,428	4,249	9,860	2,089
YALE	LMb+	743	69	2,513	11,927	182	6,503	176
YORK	LB+	224	34	1,523	44,858	9,150	3,935	1,987

+ - See Footnotes
L - Includes Law Library
M - Includes Medical Library

B - Includes branch campuses
b - Basis of volume count is bibliographic
. - Unavailable, not applicable or no data supplied

FACULTY AND ENROLLMENT
Summary Data

	Doctor's Degrees Awarded 23	Doctor's Degree Fields 24	Faculty 25	Total Students (Full-time) 26	Total Students (Part-time) 27	Graduate Students (Full-time) 28	Graudate Students (Part-time) 29
Median	590	63	1,442	25,084	3,990	5,774	2,080
High	1,964	488	5,927	73,567	19,695	18,486	8,414
Low	30	17	606	6,185	0	1,985	0
Totals	76,631	8,428	204,144	3,102,802	578,669	721,527	272,174
Number of Libraries Reporting	115	113	115	115	115	115	115

THIS PAGE INTENTIONALLY LEFT BLANK

RANK ORDER TABLES OF UNIVERSITY LIBRARIES

2013–2014

SUMMARY OF RANK ORDER TABLES FOR UNIVERSITY LIBRARIES, 2013–2014

The table below presents the rank for each university library in each of the 12 categories for which rank order tables are prepared. The table numbers in the chart below refer to the data categories listed below. The number of libraries indicates the number of ARL university libraries supplying data in each category.

Table	Data Category	Number of Libraries Reporting
1	Volumes In Library	115
2	Titles Held	113
3	Total Library Materials Expenditures	115
4	Total Salaries & Wages Expenditures	115
5	Other Operating Expenditures	115
6	Total Library Expenditures	115
7	Total Items Loaned (ILL/DD)	114
8	Total Items Borrowed (ILL/DD)	114
9	Professional Staff (FTE)	115
10	Support Staff (FTE)	115
11	Total Staff (FTE)	115
12	Library Investment Index	115

Summary of Rank Order Tables for University Libraries, 2013–2014

	1	2	3	4	5	6	7	8	9	10	11	12
ALABAMA	60	50	68	88	81	81	89	101	54	92	69	79
ALBERTA	17	34	14	29	38	26	43	87	58	14	37	26
ARIZONA	26	32	34	54	37	42	15	16	60	43	53	41
ARIZONA STATE	49	45	52	64	53	57	36	37	86	33	70	59
AUBURN	59	56	109	115	99	110	77	94	104	111	114	110
BOSTON	76	74	59	52	64	58	88	92	37	63	38	56
BOSTON COLLEGE	92	92	57	65	97	65	58	40	68	93	79	63
BRIGHAM YOUNG	50	41	67	37	50	45	47	53	32	103	21	45
BRITISH COLUMBIA	28	19	24	23	14	22	75	110	25	30	29	22
BROWN	38	36	60	69	57	63	38	32	69	79	82	62
CALGARY	71	65	51	27	96	41	101	79	74	27	50	42
CALIFORNIA, BERKELEY	7	4	9	7	4	6	67	82	4	36	10	6
CALIFORNIA, DAVIS	55	61	90	72	84	85	66	83	106	66	94	86
CALIFORNIA, IRVINE	82	66	85	60	87	79	94	71	94	47	76	81
CALIFORNIA, LOS ANGELES	8	2	31	6	9	10	44	36	14	8	9	12
CALIFORNIA, RIVERSIDE	67	79	115	106	67	111	102	95	115	101	111	112
CALIFORNIA, SAN DIEGO	34	33	80	32	28	43	85	84	33	46	40	46
CALIFORNIA, SANTA BARBARA	96	8	111	82	43	99	100	30	110	71	97	101
CASE WESTERN RESERVE	93	88	101	109	85	105	49	61	91	113	111	105
CHICAGO	9	14	16	34	41	28	12	21	69	13	34	28
CINCINNATI	57	57	73	77	83	80	27	51	46	108	84	78
COLORADO	20	20	64	71	82	72	5	35	74	56	60	73
COLORADO STATE	113	108	100	92	89	100	6	7	79	84	86	102
COLUMBIA	6	5	4	5	22	5	17	15	2	10	6	4
CONNECTICUT	72	80	70	51	104	68	31	9	58	101	62	67
CORNELL	14	13	11	9	17	12	19	14	7	12	11	11
DARTMOUTH	85	77	69	74	76	75	22	43	82	52	70	75
DELAWARE	91	100	72	85	80	82	76	88	88	79	92	82
DUKE	21	18	18	26	2	11	45	29	11	53	32	13
EMORY	65	62	23	25	18	24	54	97	23	25	25	23
FLORIDA	44	29	47	35	24	38	70	63	51	15	33	38
FLORIDA STATE	104	70	82	87	112	94	81	93	49	86	44	91
GEORGE WASHINGTON	95	98	50	45	46	46	74	13	77	56	57	48

	1	2	3	4	5	6	7	8	9	10	11	12
GEORGETOWN	46	38	35	40	54	39	29	49	41	60	51	39
GEORGIA	42	40	46	53	93	56	39	107	64	20	36	55
GEORGIA TECH	108	113	103	101	102	104	104	98	98	76	102	104
GUELPH	115	109	106	95	105	103	80	89	96	99	106	103
HARVARD	1	1	1	1	1	1	18	24	1	3	1	1
HAWAII	81	75	99	63	100	89	114	67	63	87	65	88
HOUSTON	88	89	62	90	68	78	71	80	69	93	83	77
HOWARD	99	112	112	113	115	115	112	115	113	105	110	115
ILLINOIS, CHICAGO	111	87	98	83	21	76	28	19	65	81	80	80
ILLINOIS, URBANA	2	7	15	12	26	15	4	6	13	19	16	15
INDIANA	11	11	29	30	36	29	46	27	15	31	18	29
IOWA	23	21	19	46	92	37	32	65	36	66	49	32
IOWA STATE	102	93	40	98	98	73	65	106	111	71	100	71
JOHNS HOPKINS	58	52	20	33	10	21	35	48	29	45	41	20
KANSAS	47	31	74	50	58	62	42	69	73	39	47	61
KENT STATE	89	85	113	114	110	114	111	104	98	114	113	114
KENTUCKY	52	55	66	78	66	74	72	74	45	73	59	72
LAVAL	66	105	54	57	108	66	87	111	79	28	61	66
LOUISIANA STATE	43	28	105	107	103	106	91	90	93	96	96	107
LOUISVILLE	110	110	77	103	79	95	86	81	94	99	99	93
MANITOBA	106	104	83	48	55	64	105	75	88	42	72	69
MARYLAND	62	47	63	42	34	44	82	33	22	70	39	43
MASSACHUSETTS	61	64	102	81	69	92	57	25	90	96	91	94
MCGILL	36	35	25	44	35	33	107	91	46	69	75	35
MCMASTER	112	106	87	100	106	101	110	105	102	89	104	100
MIAMI	78	68	45	56	59	51	61	99	49	47	46	51
MICHIGAN	5	6	7	4	7	4	13	11	9	2	3	5
MICHIGAN STATE	27	15	27	41	45	34	10	66	54	43	42	34
MINNESOTA	18	39	22	21	25	20	1	45	30	15	22	21
MISSOURI	48	54	95	96	62	93	25	28	98	49	78	95
MIT	101	101	78	55	70	71	59	85	48	87	84	70
MONTREAL	73	76	49	22	71	32	96	78	31	8	27	36
NEBRASKA	74	78	96	94	73	96	68	57	106	56	86	96

	1	2	3	4	5	6	7	8	9	10	11	12
NEW MEXICO	83	44	84	67	32	69	60	26	96	40	57	74
NEW YORK	29	24	5	11	11	7	79	41	3	26	13	7
NORTH CAROLINA	19	30	32	20	33	27	20	58	28	18	19	27
NORTH CAROLINA STATE	45	86	71	36	13	36	97	50	27	76	45	37
NORTHWESTERN	30	25	30	28	42	30	37	17	21	33	23	30
NOTRE DAME	53	51	43	49	63	48	55	52	38	55	54	47
OHIO	84	72	114	111	91	113	33	23	106	107	109	113
OHIO STATE	15	17	17	18	8	14	3	2	16	22	2	14
OKLAHOMA	31	46	36	86	49	54	14	42	77	63	55	53
OKLAHOMA STATE	69	60	92	99	52	91	48	77	86	95	73	92
OREGON	90	103	104	61	75	87	11	8	54	73	56	89
OTTAWA	86	84	39	66	61	52	99	109	103	50	93	52
PENNSYLVANIA	22	22	21	17	15	16	7	1	18	11	15	17
PENNSYLVANIA STATE	24	23	13	8	12	8	9	18	7	1	5	8
PITTSBURGH	25	26	26	43	44	35	23	64	34	31	35	33
PRINCETON	16	16	6	16	27	13	24	22	18	17	20	10
PURDUE	75	82	42	76	29	49	64	55	62	78	63	50
QUEEN'S	97	81	91	91	101	98	109	114	111	81	105	97
RICE	103	94	75	108	107	102	93	96	83	106	108	99
ROCHESTER	64	69	76	84	40	77	92	70	51	104	77	76
RUTGERS	37	67	38	10	51	23	16	10	35	6	14	24
SASKATCHEWAN	105	107	58	70	77	67	113	112	91	84	98	65
SOUTH CAROLINA	32	91	89	80	16	61	90	73	66	62	43	64
SOUTHERN CALIFORNIA	35	43	10	19	31	17	50	72	26	33	24	16
SOUTHERN ILLINOIS	87	97	107	110	111	109	21	31	109	98	102	109
SUNY-ALBANY	107	111	110	105	114	112	95	54	83	111	107	111
SUNY-BUFFALO	68	53	88	68	90	84	62	44	44	109	88	84
SUNY-STONY BROOK	114	102	97	112	113	108	84	108	83	115	114	106
SYRACUSE	70	71	79	73	88	83	63	76	60	54	66	83
TEMPLE	54	59	61	79	60	70	69	62	66	89	74	68
TENNESSEE	79	90	33	58	95	50	56	86	42	40	48	49
TEXAS	10	12	12	13	6	9	34	56	18	7	12	9
TEXAS A&M	40	37	8	31	30	19	30	12	17	38	27	18

SUMMARY OF RANK ORDER TABLES FOR UNIVERSITY LIBRARIES, 2013–2014

	1	2	3	4	5	6	7	8	9	10	11	12
TEXAS TECH	80	114	37	47	47	40	41	34	39	29	31	40
TORONTO	3	9	3	3	3	3	52	103	10	4	4	3
TULANE	56	73	56	102	94	86	103	100	98	73	90	85
UTAH	77	58	94	38	39	55	51	60	57	20	30	60
VANDERBILT	51	49	55	62	56	59	78	68	51	63	68	57
VIRGINIA	33	27	53	24	23	31	53	38	23	24	26	31
VIRGINIA TECH	94	99	86	97	65	90	98	47	79	81	80	90
WASHINGTON	13	UA	28	15	20	18	40	5	12	23	17	19
WASHINGTON STATE	100	95	108	104	109	107	UA	39	105	89	101	108
WASHINGTON U.-ST. LOUIS	41	42	41	59	48	47	26	20	39	59	52	44
WATERLOO	109	96	93	93	86	97	83	59	113	66	95	98
WAYNE STATE	98	83	81	89	74	88	73	46	43	109	63	87
WESTERN	39	48	44	75	72	60	106	102	72	61	89	58
WISCONSIN	12	10	48	14	19	25	2	4	6	37	8	25
YALE	4	3	2	2	5	2	8	3	5	5	7	2
YORK	63	63	65	39	78	53	108	113	74	50	66	54

Rank Order Table 1: Volumes in Library

		Value				Value
1	HARVARD	19,848,652	58	JOHNS HOPKINS		4,460,406
2	ILLINOIS, URBANA	14,072,988	59	AUBURN		4,416,728
3	TORONTO	13,923,039	60	ALABAMA		4,391,464
4	YALE	13,547,882	61	MASSACHUSETTS		4,351,859
5	MICHIGAN	13,250,648	62	MARYLAND		4,328,653
6	COLUMBIA	13,119,661	63	YORK		4,325,241
7	CALIFORNIA, BERKELEY	12,548,223	64	ROCHESTER		4,207,872
8	CALIFORNIA, LOS ANGELES	12,007,941	65	EMORY		4,184,484
9	CHICAGO	11,560,575	66	LAVAL		4,180,577
10	TEXAS	11,393,355	67	CALIFORNIA, RIVERSIDE		4,134,518
11	INDIANA	9,934,302	68	SUNY-BUFFALO		4,130,967
12	WISCONSIN	9,575,506	69	OKLAHOMA STATE		4,104,776
13	WASHINGTON	9,463,768	70	SYRACUSE		4,039,493
14	CORNELL	9,198,958	71	CALGARY		3,945,194
15	OHIO STATE	8,926,559	72	CONNECTICUT		3,923,364
16	PRINCETON	8,663,694	73	MONTREAL		3,814,783
17	ALBERTA	8,398,944	74	NEBRASKA		3,791,910
18	MINNESOTA	8,256,400	75	PURDUE		3,747,273
19	NORTH CAROLINA	7,814,952	76	BOSTON		3,688,478
20	COLORADO	7,641,471	77	UTAH		3,671,129
21	DUKE	7,607,727	78	MIAMI		3,610,359
22	PENNSYLVANIA	7,410,549	79	TENNESSEE		3,522,904
23	IOWA	7,311,554	80	TEXAS TECH		3,478,869
24	PENNSYLVANIA STATE	7,281,750	81	HAWAII		3,466,292
25	PITTSBURGH	7,124,077	82	CALIFORNIA, IRVINE		3,430,327
26	ARIZONA	6,877,849	83	NEW MEXICO		3,389,401
27	MICHIGAN STATE	6,721,988	84	OHIO		3,386,986
28	BRITISH COLUMBIA	6,631,545	85	DARTMOUTH		3,363,205
29	NEW YORK	6,253,028	86	OTTAWA		3,360,829
30	NORTHWESTERN	6,251,124	87	SOUTHERN ILLINOIS		3,360,046
31	OKLAHOMA	6,116,152	88	HOUSTON		3,352,322
32	SOUTH CAROLINA	5,679,527	89	KENT STATE		3,316,723
33	VIRGINIA	5,655,334	90	OREGON		3,245,882
34	CALIFORNIA, SAN DIEGO	5,583,014	91	DELAWARE		3,235,685
35	SOUTHERN CALIFORNIA	5,571,398	92	BOSTON COLLEGE		3,174,742
36	MCGILL	5,486,918	93	CASE WESTERN RESERVE		3,173,419
37	RUTGERS	5,455,299	94	VIRGINIA TECH		3,147,160
38	BROWN	5,415,232	95	GEORGE WASHINGTON		3,134,858
39	WESTERN	5,271,741	96	CALIFORNIA, SANTA BARBARA		3,123,554
40	TEXAS A&M	5,173,340	97	QUEEN'S		3,119,094
41	WASHINGTON U.-ST. LOUIS	5,128,983	98	WAYNE STATE		2,976,886
42	GEORGIA	5,089,626	99	HOWARD		2,947,284
43	LOUISIANA STATE	5,038,796	100	WASHINGTON STATE		2,946,984
44	FLORIDA	5,021,000	101	MIT		2,881,988
45	NORTH CAROLINA STATE	4,919,705	102	IOWA STATE		2,858,602
46	GEORGETOWN	4,798,606	103	RICE		2,842,929
47	KANSAS	4,693,070	104	FLORIDA STATE		2,836,043
48	MISSOURI	4,682,304	105	SASKATCHEWAN		2,669,043
49	ARIZONA STATE	4,669,306	106	MANITOBA		2,519,848
50	BRIGHAM YOUNG	4,633,306	107	SUNY-ALBANY		2,511,510
51	VANDERBILT	4,614,805	108	GEORGIA TECH		2,489,518
52	KENTUCKY	4,608,331	109	WATERLOO		2,487,344
53	NOTRE DAME	4,591,712	110	LOUISVILLE		2,332,386
54	TEMPLE	4,584,591	111	ILLINOIS, CHICAGO		2,315,361
55	CALIFORNIA, DAVIS	4,510,293	112	MCMASTER		2,253,025
56	TULANE	4,479,101	113	COLORADO STATE		2,245,807
57	CINCINNATI	4,473,475	114	SUNY-STONY BROOK		2,209,471
			115	GUELPH		2,021,024

Rank Order Table 2: Titles Held

		Value				Value
1	HARVARD	14,195,095	58	UTAH	3,448,961
2	CALIFORNIA, LOS ANGELES	11,898,411	59	TEMPLE	3,446,686
3	YALE	10,695,257	60	OKLAHOMA STATE	3,438,141
4	CALIFORNIA, BERKELEY	10,114,791	61	CALIFORNIA, DAVIS	3,401,755
5	COLUMBIA	9,022,370	62	EMORY	3,378,987
6	MICHIGAN	8,690,613	63	YORK	3,348,325
7	ILLINOIS, URBANA	8,383,821	64	MASSACHUSETTS	3,310,591
8	CALIFORNIA, SANTA BARBARA	8,046,138	65	CALGARY	3,165,928
9	TORONTO	8,041,704	66	CALIFORNIA, IRVINE	3,155,263
10	WISCONSIN	7,437,916	67	RUTGERS	3,146,048
11	INDIANA	7,234,398	68	MIAMI	3,105,352
12	TEXAS	7,095,417	69	ROCHESTER	3,087,086
13	CORNELL	6,948,123	70	FLORIDA STATE	3,067,049
14	CHICAGO	6,860,280	71	SYRACUSE	3,041,584
15	MICHIGAN STATE	6,695,099	72	OHIO	3,035,871
16	PRINCETON	6,257,295	73	TULANE	2,976,484
17	OHIO STATE	6,075,215	74	BOSTON	2,924,255
18	DUKE	5,898,837	75	HAWAII	2,895,212
19	BRITISH COLUMBIA	5,698,583	76	MONTREAL	2,857,474
20	COLORADO	5,404,282	77	DARTMOUTH	2,829,616
21	IOWA	5,376,505	78	NEBRASKA	2,700,142
22	PENNSYLVANIA	5,337,449	79	CALIFORNIA, RIVERSIDE	2,663,262
23	PENNSYLVANIA STATE	5,336,986	80	CONNECTICUT	2,641,242
24	NEW YORK	5,304,562	81	QUEEN'S	2,622,287
25	NORTHWESTERN	5,286,321	82	PURDUE	2,587,047
26	PITTSBURGH	5,218,300	83	WAYNE STATE	2,583,935
27	VIRGINIA	5,197,490	84	OTTAWA	2,565,867
28	LOUISIANA STATE	5,125,306	85	KENT STATE	2,559,662
29	FLORIDA	4,933,357	86	NORTH CAROLINA STATE	2,551,636
30	NORTH CAROLINA	4,877,368	87	ILLINOIS, CHICAGO	2,534,801
31	KANSAS	4,813,780	88	CASE WESTERN RESERVE	2,527,723
32	ARIZONA	4,796,552	89	HOUSTON	2,516,360
33	CALIFORNIA, SAN DIEGO	4,713,846	90	TENNESSEE	2,494,291
34	ALBERTA	4,463,667	91	SOUTH CAROLINA	2,489,688
35	MCGILL	4,392,826	92	BOSTON COLLEGE	2,463,662
36	BROWN	4,161,965	93	IOWA STATE	2,421,622
37	TEXAS A&M	4,109,075	94	RICE	2,407,628
38	GEORGETOWN	4,055,631	95	WASHINGTON STATE	2,378,138
39	MINNESOTA	4,034,731	96	WATERLOO	2,361,400
40	GEORGIA	4,024,380	97	SOUTHERN ILLINOIS	2,315,485
41	BRIGHAM YOUNG	4,016,365	98	GEORGE WASHINGTON	2,314,270
42	WASHINGTON U.-ST. LOUIS	4,006,376	99	VIRGINIA TECH	2,279,339
43	SOUTHERN CALIFORNIA	3,991,257	100	DELAWARE	2,253,730
44	NEW MEXICO	3,973,114	101	MIT	2,192,182
45	ARIZONA STATE	3,961,127	102	SUNY-STONY BROOK	2,182,148
46	OKLAHOMA	3,939,771	103	OREGON	2,145,929
47	MARYLAND	3,909,206	104	MANITOBA	2,085,532
48	WESTERN	3,886,093	105	LAVAL	2,036,697
49	VANDERBILT	3,861,552	106	MCMASTER	1,997,052
50	ALABAMA	3,841,736	107	SASKATCHEWAN	1,919,329
51	NOTRE DAME	3,734,225	108	COLORADO STATE	1,885,182
52	JOHNS HOPKINS	3,731,332	109	GUELPH	1,847,444
53	SUNY-BUFFALO	3,646,471	110	LOUISVILLE	1,660,906
54	MISSOURI	3,610,590	111	SUNY-ALBANY	1,602,005
55	KENTUCKY	3,501,066	112	HOWARD	1,352,528
56	AUBURN	3,492,354	113	GEORGIA TECH	1,098,890
57	CINCINNATI	3,484,607	114	TEXAS TECH	796,729
				WASHINGTON	

RANK ORDER TABLE 3: TOTAL LIBRARY MATERIALS EXPENDITURES

		Value			Value
1	HARVARD	44,854,018	58	SASKATCHEWAN	11,708,485
2	YALE	38,783,883	59	BOSTON	11,590,533
3	TORONTO	29,724,687	60	BROWN	11,511,759
4	COLUMBIA	29,500,049	61	TEMPLE	11,511,310
5	NEW YORK	27,275,816	62	HOUSTON	11,419,248
6	PRINCETON	25,837,011	63	MARYLAND	11,400,148
7	MICHIGAN	25,459,121	64	COLORADO	11,200,366
8	TEXAS A&M	23,609,080	65	YORK	10,995,381
9	CALIFORNIA, BERKELEY	22,726,792	66	KENTUCKY	10,976,643
10	SOUTHERN CALIFORNIA	22,428,916	67	BRIGHAM YOUNG	10,961,990
11	CORNELL	21,560,997	68	ALABAMA	10,887,008
12	TEXAS	20,922,649	69	DARTMOUTH	10,695,121
13	PENNSYLVANIA STATE	20,287,723	70	CONNECTICUT	10,693,308
14	ALBERTA	19,743,693	71	NORTH CAROLINA STATE	10,679,211
15	ILLINOIS, URBANA	19,212,701	72	DELAWARE	10,469,873
16	CHICAGO	19,176,653	73	CINCINNATI	10,177,665
17	OHIO STATE	18,977,914	74	KANSAS	10,131,719
18	DUKE	18,720,375	75	RICE	9,946,063
19	IOWA	18,603,258	76	ROCHESTER	9,944,292
20	JOHNS HOPKINS	18,496,385	77	LOUISVILLE	9,924,829
21	PENNSYLVANIA	18,385,481	78	MIT	9,876,035
22	MINNESOTA	17,963,662	79	SYRACUSE	9,570,554
23	EMORY	17,697,641	80	CALIFORNIA, SAN DIEGO	9,566,270
24	BRITISH COLUMBIA	16,763,126	81	WAYNE STATE	9,463,490
25	MCGILL	16,657,221	82	FLORIDA STATE	9,440,934
26	PITTSBURGH	16,617,295	83	MANITOBA	9,405,558
27	MICHIGAN STATE	16,308,972	84	NEW MEXICO	9,341,631
28	WASHINGTON	16,067,994	85	CALIFORNIA, IRVINE	9,318,324
29	INDIANA	16,027,788	86	VIRGINIA TECH	9,161,016
30	NORTHWESTERN	15,702,473	87	MCMASTER	9,111,792
31	CALIFORNIA, LOS ANGELES	15,610,465	88	SUNY-BUFFALO	9,065,327
32	NORTH CAROLINA	15,557,364	89	SOUTH CAROLINA	8,941,910
33	TENNESSEE	14,781,177	90	CALIFORNIA, DAVIS	8,940,658
34	ARIZONA	14,660,978	91	QUEEN'S	8,921,980
35	GEORGETOWN	14,399,422	92	OKLAHOMA STATE	8,882,554
36	OKLAHOMA	14,299,029	93	WATERLOO	8,864,282
37	TEXAS TECH	14,256,641	94	UTAH	8,796,235
38	RUTGERS	14,110,365	95	MISSOURI	8,660,675
39	OTTAWA	13,959,115	96	NEBRASKA	8,618,714
40	IOWA STATE	13,756,647	97	SUNY-STONY BROOK	8,401,621
41	WASHINGTON U.-ST. LOUIS	13,711,438	98	ILLINOIS, CHICAGO	8,053,918
42	PURDUE	13,428,913	99	HAWAII	7,856,488
43	NOTRE DAME	13,352,304	100	COLORADO STATE	7,823,526
44	WESTERN	13,289,824	101	CASE WESTERN RESERVE	7,656,923
45	MIAMI	13,280,160	102	MASSACHUSETTS	7,571,461
46	GEORGIA	12,831,691	103	GEORGIA TECH	7,474,554
47	FLORIDA	12,827,981	104	OREGON	7,443,692
48	WISCONSIN	12,797,066	105	LOUISIANA STATE	7,208,499
49	MONTREAL	12,510,606	106	GUELPH	7,160,715
50	GEORGE WASHINGTON	12,193,022	107	SOUTHERN ILLINOIS	6,948,240
51	CALGARY	12,140,520	108	WASHINGTON STATE	6,847,684
52	ARIZONA STATE	12,123,498	109	AUBURN	6,594,618
53	VIRGINIA	12,109,120	110	SUNY-ALBANY	6,033,091
54	LAVAL	11,952,746	111	CALIFORNIA, SANTA BARBARA	5,860,806
55	VANDERBILT	11,950,301	112	HOWARD	5,769,950
56	TULANE	11,913,606	113	KENT STATE	5,381,081
57	BOSTON COLLEGE	11,902,501	114	OHIO	4,993,681
			115	CALIFORNIA, RIVERSIDE	4,424,542

Rank Order Table 4: Total Salaries & Wages Expenditures

		Value				Value
1	HARVARD	59,113,672		58	TENNESSEE	10,219,802
2	YALE	37,973,327		59	WASHINGTON U.-ST. LOUIS	10,208,127
3	TORONTO	37,545,305		60	CALIFORNIA, IRVINE	10,135,792
4	MICHIGAN	33,922,216		61	OREGON	9,989,312
5	COLUMBIA	31,607,063		62	VANDERBILT	9,972,648
6	CALIFORNIA, LOS ANGELES	27,728,222		63	HAWAII	9,968,725
7	CALIFORNIA, BERKELEY	26,980,912		64	ARIZONA STATE	9,935,115
8	PENNSYLVANIA STATE	26,558,591		65	BOSTON COLLEGE	9,930,357
9	CORNELL	23,986,642		66	OTTAWA	9,598,213
10	RUTGERS	23,916,544		67	NEW MEXICO	9,533,839
11	NEW YORK	23,906,160		68	SUNY-BUFFALO	9,490,524
12	ILLINOIS, URBANA	22,549,786		69	BROWN	9,423,968
13	TEXAS	22,317,216		70	SASKATCHEWAN	9,323,336
14	WISCONSIN	20,868,378		71	COLORADO	9,244,867
15	WASHINGTON	20,841,881		72	CALIFORNIA, DAVIS	9,160,816
16	PRINCETON	20,752,134		73	SYRACUSE	9,075,096
17	PENNSYLVANIA	20,621,052		74	DARTMOUTH	9,062,060
18	OHIO STATE	19,790,061		75	WESTERN	9,000,822
19	SOUTHERN CALIFORNIA	18,763,146		76	PURDUE	8,982,400
20	NORTH CAROLINA	18,731,906		77	CINCINNATI	8,737,069
21	MINNESOTA	18,653,609		78	KENTUCKY	8,709,042
22	MONTREAL	18,365,838		79	TEMPLE	8,692,742
23	BRITISH COLUMBIA	17,727,662		80	SOUTH CAROLINA	8,654,362
24	VIRGINIA	17,053,495		81	MASSACHUSETTS	8,584,426
25	EMORY	16,165,758		82	CALIFORNIA, SANTA BARBARA	8,436,162
26	DUKE	15,841,735		83	ILLINOIS, CHICAGO	8,112,088
27	CALGARY	15,367,141		84	ROCHESTER	8,111,516
28	NORTHWESTERN	15,265,127		85	DELAWARE	8,110,343
29	ALBERTA	14,889,441		86	OKLAHOMA	7,881,309
30	INDIANA	14,801,772		87	FLORIDA STATE	7,855,731
31	TEXAS A&M	14,276,051		88	ALABAMA	7,847,337
32	CALIFORNIA, SAN DIEGO	14,097,968		89	WAYNE STATE	7,744,786
33	JOHNS HOPKINS	14,074,705		90	HOUSTON	7,586,149
34	CHICAGO	13,806,193		91	QUEEN'S	7,581,395
35	FLORIDA	13,643,423		92	COLORADO STATE	7,434,683
36	NORTH CAROLINA STATE	13,469,704		93	WATERLOO	7,412,323
37	BRIGHAM YOUNG	13,459,762		94	NEBRASKA	7,318,148
38	UTAH	12,912,778		95	GUELPH	7,307,099
39	YORK	12,868,863		96	MISSOURI	7,198,027
40	GEORGETOWN	12,688,994		97	VIRGINIA TECH	7,140,129
41	MICHIGAN STATE	12,655,783		98	IOWA STATE	6,942,790
42	MARYLAND	12,632,570		99	OKLAHOMA STATE	6,689,091
43	PITTSBURGH	12,105,408		100	MCMASTER	6,530,598
44	MCGILL	11,953,042		101	GEORGIA TECH	6,472,220
45	GEORGE WASHINGTON	11,887,219		102	TULANE	6,344,619
46	IOWA	11,883,298		103	LOUISVILLE	6,236,500
47	TEXAS TECH	11,810,949		104	WASHINGTON STATE	6,205,117
48	MANITOBA	11,299,862		105	SUNY-ALBANY	5,913,708
49	NOTRE DAME	11,183,546		106	CALIFORNIA, RIVERSIDE	5,845,948
50	KANSAS	10,936,163		107	LOUISIANA STATE	5,833,398
51	CONNECTICUT	10,932,537		108	RICE	5,579,013
52	BOSTON	10,854,206		109	CASE WESTERN RESERVE	5,494,541
53	GEORGIA	10,738,365		110	SOUTHERN ILLINOIS	5,292,410
54	ARIZONA	10,461,126		111	OHIO	5,064,842
55	MIT	10,450,374		112	SUNY-STONY BROOK	4,831,659
56	MIAMI	10,285,400		113	HOWARD	4,761,220
57	LAVAL	10,231,488		114	KENT STATE	4,725,057
				115	AUBURN	4,709,273

Rank Order Table 5: Other Operating Expenditures

		Value				Value
1	HARVARD	19,167,565		58	KANSAS	2,430,660
2	DUKE	17,545,307		59	MIAMI	2,397,729
3	TORONTO	13,551,856		60	TEMPLE	2,339,353
4	CALIFORNIA, BERKELEY	12,951,485		61	OTTAWA	2,316,610
5	YALE	10,828,300		62	MISSOURI	2,273,789
6	TEXAS	10,647,359		63	NOTRE DAME	2,238,097
7	MICHIGAN	10,381,986		64	BOSTON	2,214,384
8	OHIO STATE	9,853,452		65	VIRGINIA TECH	2,178,622
9	CALIFORNIA, LOS ANGELES	9,427,546		66	KENTUCKY	2,171,585
10	JOHNS HOPKINS	8,676,400		67	CALIFORNIA, RIVERSIDE	2,111,241
11	NEW YORK	8,399,666		68	HOUSTON	2,092,779
12	PENNSYLVANIA STATE	7,902,069		69	MASSACHUSETTS	2,054,907
13	NORTH CAROLINA STATE	7,730,527		70	MIT	2,033,098
14	BRITISH COLUMBIA	6,533,506		71	MONTREAL	1,987,081
15	PENNSYLVANIA	6,501,490		72	WESTERN	1,970,950
16	SOUTH CAROLINA	6,487,475		73	NEBRASKA	1,958,039
17	CORNELL	6,195,913		74	WAYNE STATE	1,954,637
18	EMORY	6,161,784		75	OREGON	1,935,585
19	WISCONSIN	5,698,427		76	DARTMOUTH	1,889,546
20	WASHINGTON	5,690,848		77	SASKATCHEWAN	1,840,796
21	ILLINOIS, CHICAGO	5,399,924		78	YORK	1,781,070
22	COLUMBIA	5,325,286		79	LOUISVILLE	1,769,972
23	VIRGINIA	4,997,620		80	DELAWARE	1,768,688
24	FLORIDA	4,736,497		81	ALABAMA	1,655,547
25	MINNESOTA	4,735,995		82	COLORADO	1,643,291
26	ILLINOIS, URBANA	4,716,983		83	CINCINNATI	1,639,131
27	PRINCETON	4,683,216		84	CALIFORNIA, DAVIS	1,602,610
28	CALIFORNIA, SAN DIEGO	4,197,168		85	CASE WESTERN RESERVE	1,598,538
29	PURDUE	4,085,003		86	WATERLOO	1,577,443
30	TEXAS A&M	4,057,764		87	CALIFORNIA, IRVINE	1,550,253
31	SOUTHERN CALIFORNIA	3,944,160		88	SYRACUSE	1,512,432
32	NEW MEXICO	3,783,040		89	COLORADO STATE	1,488,479
33	NORTH CAROLINA	3,731,461		90	SUNY-BUFFALO	1,405,801
34	MARYLAND	3,712,597		91	OHIO	1,371,906
35	MCGILL	3,703,497		92	IOWA	1,370,969
36	INDIANA	3,658,049		93	GEORGIA	1,345,227
37	ARIZONA	3,644,219		94	TULANE	1,317,445
38	ALBERTA	3,533,440		95	TENNESSEE	1,291,992
39	UTAH	3,417,100		96	CALGARY	1,277,863
40	ROCHESTER	3,412,424		97	BOSTON COLLEGE	1,277,431
41	CHICAGO	3,409,443		98	IOWA STATE	1,250,361
42	NORTHWESTERN	3,346,325		99	AUBURN	1,214,482
43	CALIFORNIA, SANTA BARBARA	3,287,609		100	HAWAII	1,147,083
44	PITTSBURGH	3,225,860		101	QUEEN'S	1,126,671
45	MICHIGAN STATE	3,182,686		102	GEORGIA TECH	1,125,202
46	GEORGE WASHINGTON	3,143,363		103	LOUISIANA STATE	1,073,412
47	TEXAS TECH	3,104,400		104	CONNECTICUT	1,035,808
48	WASHINGTON U.-ST. LOUIS	3,102,065		105	GUELPH	977,447
49	OKLAHOMA	3,091,723		106	MCMASTER	906,594
50	BRIGHAM YOUNG	3,059,592		107	RICE	863,558
51	RUTGERS	2,874,076		108	LAVAL	738,588
52	OKLAHOMA STATE	2,808,106		109	WASHINGTON STATE	721,711
53	ARIZONA STATE	2,806,112		110	KENT STATE	709,690
54	GEORGETOWN	2,781,056		111	SOUTHERN ILLINOIS	655,901
55	MANITOBA	2,603,641		112	FLORIDA STATE	634,803
56	VANDERBILT	2,570,105		113	SUNY-STONY BROOK	457,931
57	BROWN	2,536,908		114	SUNY-ALBANY	430,984
				115	HOWARD	134,210

Rank Order Table 6: Total Library Expenditures

		Value				Value
1	HARVARD	123,135,255		58	BOSTON	24,659,123
2	YALE	87,585,510		59	VANDERBILT	24,493,054
3	TORONTO	80,821,848		60	WESTERN	24,261,596
4	MICHIGAN	69,763,323		61	SOUTH CAROLINA	24,083,747
5	COLUMBIA	66,432,398		62	KANSAS	23,498,542
6	CALIFORNIA, BERKELEY	62,659,189		63	BROWN	23,472,635
7	NEW YORK	59,581,642		64	MANITOBA	23,309,060
8	PENNSYLVANIA STATE	54,748,383		65	BOSTON COLLEGE	23,110,289
9	TEXAS	53,887,224		66	LAVAL	22,922,822
10	CALIFORNIA, LOS ANGELES	52,766,233		67	SASKATCHEWAN	22,872,616
11	DUKE	52,107,417		68	CONNECTICUT	22,661,653
12	CORNELL	51,743,552		69	NEW MEXICO	22,658,510
13	PRINCETON	51,272,361		70	TEMPLE	22,543,405
14	OHIO STATE	48,621,427		71	MIT	22,359,507
15	ILLINOIS, URBANA	46,479,470		72	COLORADO	22,088,524
16	PENNSYLVANIA	45,508,023		73	IOWA STATE	21,949,798
17	SOUTHERN CALIFORNIA	45,136,222		74	KENTUCKY	21,857,270
18	WASHINGTON	42,600,723		75	DARTMOUTH	21,646,727
19	TEXAS A&M	41,942,895		76	ILLINOIS, CHICAGO	21,565,930
20	MINNESOTA	41,353,266		77	ROCHESTER	21,468,232
21	JOHNS HOPKINS	41,247,490		78	HOUSTON	21,098,176
22	BRITISH COLUMBIA	41,024,295		79	CALIFORNIA, IRVINE	21,004,369
23	RUTGERS	40,900,985		80	CINCINNATI	20,553,865
24	EMORY	40,025,183		81	ALABAMA	20,389,892
25	WISCONSIN	39,363,871		82	DELAWARE	20,348,904
26	ALBERTA	38,166,575		83	SYRACUSE	20,158,082
27	NORTH CAROLINA	38,020,731		84	SUNY-BUFFALO	19,961,652
28	CHICAGO	36,392,289		85	CALIFORNIA, DAVIS	19,704,084
29	INDIANA	34,487,609		86	TULANE	19,575,670
30	NORTHWESTERN	34,313,925		87	OREGON	19,368,589
31	VIRGINIA	34,160,235		88	WAYNE STATE	19,162,913
32	MONTREAL	32,863,525		89	HAWAII	18,972,296
33	MCGILL	32,313,761		90	VIRGINIA TECH	18,479,767
34	MICHIGAN STATE	32,147,441		91	OKLAHOMA STATE	18,379,751
35	PITTSBURGH	31,948,563		92	MASSACHUSETTS	18,210,794
36	NORTH CAROLINA STATE	31,879,442		93	MISSOURI	18,132,491
37	IOWA	31,857,525		94	FLORIDA STATE	17,931,468
38	FLORIDA	31,207,901		95	LOUISVILLE	17,931,301
39	GEORGETOWN	29,869,472		96	NEBRASKA	17,894,901
40	TEXAS TECH	29,171,990		97	WATERLOO	17,854,047
41	CALGARY	28,785,524		98	QUEEN'S	17,630,047
42	ARIZONA	28,766,323		99	CALIFORNIA, SANTA BARBARA	17,584,577
43	CALIFORNIA, SAN DIEGO	27,861,406		100	COLORADO STATE	16,746,688
44	MARYLAND	27,745,315		101	MCMASTER	16,548,985
45	BRIGHAM YOUNG	27,481,344		102	RICE	16,388,634
46	GEORGE WASHINGTON	27,223,604		103	GUELPH	15,445,261
47	WASHINGTON U.-ST. LOUIS	27,021,630		104	GEORGIA TECH	15,071,976
48	NOTRE DAME	26,773,947		105	CASE WESTERN RESERVE	14,750,002
49	PURDUE	26,496,316		106	LOUISIANA STATE	14,115,309
50	TENNESSEE	26,292,971		107	WASHINGTON STATE	13,774,512
51	MIAMI	25,963,289		108	SUNY-STONY BROOK	13,691,211
52	OTTAWA	25,873,938		109	SOUTHERN ILLINOIS	12,896,551
53	YORK	25,645,315		110	AUBURN	12,518,373
54	OKLAHOMA	25,272,061		111	CALIFORNIA, RIVERSIDE	12,381,731
55	UTAH	25,126,113		112	SUNY-ALBANY	12,377,783
56	GEORGIA	24,915,283		113	OHIO	11,430,429
57	ARIZONA STATE	24,864,725		114	KENT STATE	10,815,828
				115	HOWARD	10,665,380

Rank Order Table 7: Total Items Loaned (ILL/DD)

		Value				Value
1	MINNESOTA	131,918		58	BOSTON COLLEGE	28,195
2	WISCONSIN	125,502		59	MIT	27,836
3	OHIO STATE	106,507		60	NEW MEXICO	27,835
4	ILLINOIS, URBANA	86,226		61	MIAMI	27,607
5	COLORADO	82,629		62	SUNY-BUFFALO	27,571
6	COLORADO STATE	82,192		63	SYRACUSE	27,511
7	PENNSYLVANIA	79,297		64	PURDUE	27,306
8	YALE	74,958		65	IOWA STATE	27,138
9	PENNSYLVANIA STATE	71,572		66	CALIFORNIA, DAVIS	27,040
10	MICHIGAN STATE	69,225		67	CALIFORNIA, BERKELEY	27,009
11	OREGON	66,526		68	NEBRASKA	26,909
12	CHICAGO	63,077		69	TEMPLE	26,090
13	MICHIGAN	58,462		70	FLORIDA	26,081
14	OKLAHOMA	57,782		71	HOUSTON	25,669
15	ARIZONA	56,244		72	KENTUCKY	25,262
16	RUTGERS	55,109		73	WAYNE STATE	25,048
17	COLUMBIA	54,391		74	GEORGE WASHINGTON	24,801
18	HARVARD	52,485		75	BRITISH COLUMBIA	23,428
19	CORNELL	51,716		76	DELAWARE	23,377
20	NORTH CAROLINA	51,217		77	AUBURN	22,482
21	SOUTHERN ILLINOIS	50,318		78	VANDERBILT	21,965
22	DARTMOUTH	50,003		79	NEW YORK	21,922
23	PITTSBURGH	49,343		80	GUELPH	21,905
24	PRINCETON	48,459		81	FLORIDA STATE	21,490
25	MISSOURI	47,875		82	MARYLAND	20,651
26	WASHINGTON U.-ST. LOUIS	46,423		83	WATERLOO	20,159
27	CINCINNATI	45,656		84	SUNY-STONY BROOK	18,568
28	ILLINOIS, CHICAGO	45,406		85	CALIFORNIA, SAN DIEGO	18,270
29	GEORGETOWN	45,344		86	LOUISVILLE	18,196
30	TEXAS A&M	45,046		87	LAVAL	18,144
31	CONNECTICUT	44,074		88	BOSTON	17,189
32	IOWA	43,751		89	ALABAMA	16,603
33	OHIO	42,807		90	SOUTH CAROLINA	16,549
34	TEXAS	40,881		91	LOUISIANA STATE	16,472
35	JOHNS HOPKINS	40,480		92	ROCHESTER	16,382
36	ARIZONA STATE	39,964		93	RICE	16,289
37	NORTHWESTERN	39,687		94	CALIFORNIA, IRVINE	16,263
38	BROWN	38,806		95	SUNY-ALBANY	15,599
39	GEORGIA	38,641		96	MONTREAL	15,104
40	WASHINGTON	38,111		97	NORTH CAROLINA STATE	14,854
41	TEXAS TECH	37,271		98	VIRGINIA TECH	14,686
42	KANSAS	36,905		99	OTTAWA	14,584
43	ALBERTA	36,153		100	CALIFORNIA, SANTA BARBARA	14,016
44	CALIFORNIA, LOS ANGELES	35,703		101	CALGARY	13,842
45	DUKE	34,795		102	CALIFORNIA, RIVERSIDE	13,711
46	INDIANA	34,470		103	TULANE	13,497
47	BRIGHAM YOUNG	33,887		104	GEORGIA TECH	11,546
48	OKLAHOMA STATE	33,753		105	MANITOBA	11,386
49	CASE WESTERN RESERVE	33,507		106	WESTERN	11,176
50	SOUTHERN CALIFORNIA	32,994		107	MCGILL	10,556
51	UTAH	32,840		108	YORK	9,470
52	TORONTO	32,496		109	QUEEN'S	9,429
53	VIRGINIA	29,359		110	MCMASTER	9,181
54	EMORY	28,962		111	KENT STATE	7,475
55	NOTRE DAME	28,832		112	HOWARD	6,961
56	TENNESSEE	28,708		113	SASKATCHEWAN	5,537
57	MASSACHUSETTS	28,634		114	HAWAII	5,037
					WASHINGTON STATE	

Rank Order Table 8: Total Items Borrowed (ILL/DD)

		Value				Value
1	PENNSYLVANIA	106,494		58	NORTH CAROLINA	24,454
2	OHIO STATE	95,791		59	WATERLOO	23,644
3	YALE	87,135		60	UTAH	23,377
4	WISCONSIN	81,149		61	CASE WESTERN RESERVE	22,836
5	WASHINGTON	75,889		62	TEMPLE	22,504
6	ILLINOIS, URBANA	66,825		63	FLORIDA	21,873
7	COLORADO STATE	60,515		64	PITTSBURGH	21,474
8	OREGON	59,165		65	IOWA	21,391
9	CONNECTICUT	57,961		66	MICHIGAN STATE	21,065
10	RUTGERS	57,131		67	HAWAII	20,918
11	MICHIGAN	56,229		68	VANDERBILT	20,690
12	TEXAS A&M	51,878		69	KANSAS	20,668
13	GEORGE WASHINGTON	50,767		70	ROCHESTER	20,381
14	CORNELL	49,841		71	CALIFORNIA, IRVINE	20,305
15	COLUMBIA	48,833		72	SOUTHERN CALIFORNIA	20,164
16	ARIZONA	47,537		73	SOUTH CAROLINA	18,936
17	NORTHWESTERN	44,740		74	KENTUCKY	18,390
18	PENNSYLVANIA STATE	43,452		75	MANITOBA	18,347
19	ILLINOIS, CHICAGO	42,798		76	SYRACUSE	17,549
20	WASHINGTON U.-ST. LOUIS	41,675		77	OKLAHOMA STATE	17,394
21	CHICAGO	41,390		78	MONTREAL	17,382
22	PRINCETON	40,709		79	CALGARY	17,293
23	OHIO	39,703		80	HOUSTON	17,049
24	HARVARD	39,043		81	LOUISVILLE	16,990
25	MASSACHUSETTS	38,673		82	CALIFORNIA, BERKELEY	16,850
26	NEW MEXICO	36,678		83	CALIFORNIA, DAVIS	16,848
27	INDIANA	36,244		84	CALIFORNIA, SAN DIEGO	15,985
28	MISSOURI	36,205		85	MIT	15,935
29	DUKE	35,942		86	TENNESSEE	15,876
30	CALIFORNIA, SANTA BARBARA	35,782		87	ALBERTA	15,647
31	SOUTHERN ILLINOIS	35,743		88	DELAWARE	15,645
32	BROWN	35,737		89	GUELPH	15,533
33	MARYLAND	35,146		90	LOUISIANA STATE	14,252
34	TEXAS TECH	34,527		91	MCGILL	12,547
35	COLORADO	34,502		92	BOSTON	12,001
36	CALIFORNIA, LOS ANGELES	34,424		93	FLORIDA STATE	11,920
37	ARIZONA STATE	33,578		94	AUBURN	11,786
38	VIRGINIA	32,421		95	CALIFORNIA, RIVERSIDE	11,660
39	WASHINGTON STATE	32,266		96	RICE	11,571
40	BOSTON COLLEGE	32,015		97	EMORY	11,513
41	NEW YORK	31,975		98	GEORGIA TECH	10,989
42	OKLAHOMA	31,697		99	MIAMI	10,648
43	DARTMOUTH	31,652		100	TULANE	10,431
44	SUNY-BUFFALO	31,233		101	ALABAMA	10,176
45	MINNESOTA	31,187		102	WESTERN	9,660
46	WAYNE STATE	31,054		103	TORONTO	9,457
47	VIRGINIA TECH	30,753		104	KENT STATE	9,130
48	JOHNS HOPKINS	30,050		105	MCMASTER	9,088
49	GEORGETOWN	29,411		106	IOWA STATE	8,908
50	NORTH CAROLINA STATE	28,722		107	GEORGIA	8,807
51	CINCINNATI	28,504		108	SUNY-STONY BROOK	8,208
52	NOTRE DAME	27,739		109	OTTAWA	7,998
53	BRIGHAM YOUNG	26,291		110	BRITISH COLUMBIA	7,898
54	SUNY-ALBANY	26,156		111	LAVAL	6,310
55	PURDUE	25,508		112	SASKATCHEWAN	4,980
56	TEXAS	25,099		113	YORK	4,739
57	NEBRASKA	25,011		114	QUEEN'S	4,496
				115	HOWARD	2,513

RANK ORDER TABLE 9: PROFESSIONAL STAFF (FTE)

		Value				Value
1	HARVARD	464	58	ALBERTA		83
2	COLUMBIA	317	58	CONNECTICUT		83
3	NEW YORK	255	60	ARIZONA		82
4	CALIFORNIA, BERKELEY	247	60	SYRACUSE		82
5	YALE	243	62	PURDUE		81
6	WISCONSIN	231	63	HAWAII		80
7	CORNELL	210	64	GEORGIA		79
7	PENNSYLVANIA STATE	210	65	ILLINOIS, CHICAGO		75
9	MICHIGAN	204	66	SOUTH CAROLINA		74
10	TORONTO	192	66	TEMPLE		74
11	DUKE	189	68	BOSTON COLLEGE		73
12	WASHINGTON	181	69	BROWN		72
13	ILLINOIS, URBANA	167	69	CHICAGO		72
14	CALIFORNIA, LOS ANGELES	165	69	HOUSTON		72
15	INDIANA	152	72	WESTERN		71
16	OHIO STATE	151	73	KANSAS		70
17	TEXAS A&M	149	74	CALGARY		69
18	PENNSYLVANIA	148	74	COLORADO		69
18	PRINCETON	148	74	YORK		69
18	TEXAS	148	77	GEORGE WASHINGTON		67
21	NORTHWESTERN	140	77	OKLAHOMA		67
22	MARYLAND	138	79	COLORADO STATE		66
23	EMORY	136	79	LAVAL		66
23	VIRGINIA	136	79	VIRGINIA TECH		66
25	BRITISH COLUMBIA	135	82	DARTMOUTH		65
26	SOUTHERN CALIFORNIA	134	83	RICE		63
27	NORTH CAROLINA STATE	127	83	SUNY-ALBANY		63
28	NORTH CAROLINA	125	83	SUNY-STONY BROOK		63
29	JOHNS HOPKINS	124	86	ARIZONA STATE		61
30	MINNESOTA	117	86	OKLAHOMA STATE		61
31	MONTREAL	115	88	DELAWARE		60
32	BRIGHAM YOUNG	113	88	MANITOBA		60
33	CALIFORNIA, SAN DIEGO	111	90	MASSACHUSETTS		59
34	PITTSBURGH	110	91	CASE WESTERN RESERVE		58
35	RUTGERS	109	91	SASKATCHEWAN		58
36	IOWA	108	93	LOUISIANA STATE		57
37	BOSTON	107	94	CALIFORNIA, IRVINE		55
38	NOTRE DAME	104	94	LOUISVILLE		55
39	TEXAS TECH	103	96	GUELPH		54
39	WASHINGTON U.-ST. LOUIS	103	96	NEW MEXICO		54
41	GEORGETOWN	100	98	GEORGIA TECH		52
42	TENNESSEE	98	98	KENT STATE		52
43	WAYNE STATE	97	98	MISSOURI		52
44	SUNY-BUFFALO	94	98	TULANE		52
45	KENTUCKY	93	102	MCMASTER		49
46	CINCINNATI	92	103	OTTAWA		48
46	MCGILL	92	104	AUBURN		47
48	MIT	91	105	WASHINGTON STATE		45
49	FLORIDA STATE	88	106	CALIFORNIA, DAVIS		44
49	MIAMI	88	106	NEBRASKA		44
51	FLORIDA	87	106	OHIO		44
51	ROCHESTER	87	109	SOUTHERN ILLINOIS		42
51	VANDERBILT	87	110	CALIFORNIA, SANTA BARBARA		40
54	ALABAMA	86	111	IOWA STATE		39
54	MICHIGAN STATE	86	111	QUEEN'S		39
54	OREGON	86	113	HOWARD		37
57	UTAH	84	113	WATERLOO		37
			115	CALIFORNIA, RIVERSIDE		35

Rank Order Table 10: Support Staff (FTE)

		Value				Value
1	PENNSYLVANIA STATE	368		56	NEBRASKA	96
2	MICHIGAN	340		59	WASHINGTON U.-ST. LOUIS	95
3	HARVARD	330		60	GEORGETOWN	94
4	TORONTO	322		61	WESTERN	90
5	YALE	283		62	SOUTH CAROLINA	89
6	RUTGERS	243		63	BOSTON	88
7	TEXAS	226		63	OKLAHOMA	88
8	CALIFORNIA, LOS ANGELES	222		63	VANDERBILT	88
8	MONTREAL	222		66	CALIFORNIA, DAVIS	86
10	COLUMBIA	194		66	IOWA	86
11	PENNSYLVANIA	182		66	WATERLOO	86
12	CORNELL	181		69	MCGILL	84
13	CHICAGO	180		70	MARYLAND	83
14	ALBERTA	179		71	CALIFORNIA, SANTA BARBARA	81
15	FLORIDA	177		71	IOWA STATE	81
15	MINNESOTA	177		73	KENTUCKY	80
17	PRINCETON	171		73	OREGON	80
18	NORTH CAROLINA	169		73	TULANE	80
19	ILLINOIS, URBANA	168		76	GEORGIA TECH	79
20	GEORGIA	164		76	NORTH CAROLINA STATE	79
20	UTAH	164		78	PURDUE	78
22	OHIO STATE	162		79	BROWN	77
23	WASHINGTON	161		79	DELAWARE	77
24	VIRGINIA	160		81	ILLINOIS, CHICAGO	76
25	EMORY	155		81	QUEEN'S	76
26	NEW YORK	153		81	VIRGINIA TECH	76
27	CALGARY	152		84	COLORADO STATE	75
28	LAVAL	148		84	SASKATCHEWAN	75
29	TEXAS TECH	146		86	FLORIDA STATE	72
30	BRITISH COLUMBIA	145		87	HAWAII	71
31	INDIANA	137		87	MIT	71
31	PITTSBURGH	137		89	MCMASTER	70
33	ARIZONA STATE	134		89	TEMPLE	70
33	NORTHWESTERN	134		89	WASHINGTON STATE	70
33	SOUTHERN CALIFORNIA	134		92	ALABAMA	68
36	CALIFORNIA, BERKELEY	133		93	BOSTON COLLEGE	66
37	WISCONSIN	128		93	HOUSTON	66
38	TEXAS A&M	125		95	OKLAHOMA STATE	65
39	KANSAS	124		96	LOUISIANA STATE	64
40	NEW MEXICO	116		96	MASSACHUSETTS	64
40	TENNESSEE	116		98	SOUTHERN ILLINOIS	61
42	MANITOBA	115		99	GUELPH	60
43	ARIZONA	111		99	LOUISVILLE	60
43	MICHIGAN STATE	111		101	CALIFORNIA, RIVERSIDE	59
45	JOHNS HOPKINS	109		101	CONNECTICUT	59
46	CALIFORNIA, SAN DIEGO	108		103	BRIGHAM YOUNG	58
47	CALIFORNIA, IRVINE	106		104	ROCHESTER	56
47	MIAMI	106		105	HOWARD	51
49	MISSOURI	104		106	RICE	48
50	OTTAWA	103		107	OHIO	45
50	YORK	103		108	CINCINNATI	43
52	DARTMOUTH	102		109	SUNY-BUFFALO	40
53	DUKE	101		109	WAYNE STATE	40
54	SYRACUSE	100		111	AUBURN	33
55	NOTRE DAME	99		111	SUNY-ALBANY	33
56	COLORADO	96		113	CASE WESTERN RESERVE	32
56	GEORGE WASHINGTON	96		114	KENT STATE	18
				115	SUNY-STONY BROOK	13

Rank Order Table 11: Total Staff (FTE)

#		Value		#		Value
1	HARVARD	794		57	NEW MEXICO	221
2	OHIO STATE	686		59	KENTUCKY	218
3	MICHIGAN	669		60	COLORADO	215
4	TORONTO	647		61	LAVAL	214
5	PENNSYLVANIA STATE	633		62	CONNECTICUT	210
6	COLUMBIA	589		63	PURDUE	207
7	YALE	577		63	WAYNE STATE	207
8	WISCONSIN	545		65	HAWAII	206
9	CALIFORNIA, LOS ANGELES	504		66	SYRACUSE	200
10	CALIFORNIA, BERKELEY	500		66	YORK	200
11	CORNELL	493		68	VANDERBILT	198
12	TEXAS	486		69	ALABAMA	197
13	NEW YORK	485		70	ARIZONA STATE	195
14	RUTGERS	445		70	DARTMOUTH	195
15	PENNSYLVANIA	438		72	MANITOBA	193
16	ILLINOIS, URBANA	435		73	OKLAHOMA STATE	192
17	WASHINGTON	432		74	TEMPLE	191
18	INDIANA	397		75	MCGILL	190
19	NORTH CAROLINA	373		76	CALIFORNIA, IRVINE	189
20	PRINCETON	369		77	ROCHESTER	188
21	BRIGHAM YOUNG	367		78	MISSOURI	186
22	MINNESOTA	363		79	BOSTON COLLEGE	185
23	NORTHWESTERN	361		80	ILLINOIS, CHICAGO	182
24	SOUTHERN CALIFORNIA	356		80	VIRGINIA TECH	182
25	EMORY	348		82	BROWN	179
26	VIRGINIA	342		83	HOUSTON	178
27	MONTREAL	340		84	CINCINNATI	177
27	TEXAS A&M	340		84	MIT	177
29	BRITISH COLUMBIA	327		86	COLORADO STATE	176
30	UTAH	325		86	NEBRASKA	176
31	TEXAS TECH	320		88	SUNY-BUFFALO	174
32	DUKE	317		89	WESTERN	172
33	FLORIDA	312		90	TULANE	162
34	CHICAGO	304		91	MASSACHUSETTS	161
35	PITTSBURGH	302		92	DELAWARE	160
36	GEORGIA	293		93	OTTAWA	159
37	ALBERTA	289		94	CALIFORNIA, DAVIS	158
38	BOSTON	278		95	WATERLOO	154
39	MARYLAND	274		96	LOUISIANA STATE	152
40	CALIFORNIA, SAN DIEGO	271		97	CALIFORNIA, SANTA BARBARA	150
41	JOHNS HOPKINS	269		98	SASKATCHEWAN	147
42	MICHIGAN STATE	264		99	LOUISVILLE	145
43	SOUTH CAROLINA	262		100	IOWA STATE	143
44	FLORIDA STATE	259		101	WASHINGTON STATE	141
45	NORTH CAROLINA STATE	258		102	GEORGIA TECH	136
46	MIAMI	256		102	SOUTHERN ILLINOIS	136
47	KANSAS	253		104	MCMASTER	133
48	TENNESSEE	245		105	QUEEN'S	131
49	IOWA	243		106	GUELPH	124
50	CALGARY	242		107	SUNY-ALBANY	123
51	GEORGETOWN	238		108	RICE	120
52	WASHINGTON U.-ST. LOUIS	236		109	OHIO	119
53	ARIZONA	234		110	HOWARD	118
54	NOTRE DAME	230		111	CALIFORNIA, RIVERSIDE	117
55	OKLAHOMA	229		111	CASE WESTERN RESERVE	117
56	OREGON	227		113	KENT STATE	108
57	GEORGE WASHINGTON	221		114	AUBURN	105
				114	SUNY-STONY BROOK	105

Rank Order Table 12: Library Investment Index

		Value				Value
1	HARVARD	5.53		58	WESTERN	-0.30
2	YALE	3.44		59	ARIZONA STATE	-0.31
3	TORONTO	2.88		60	UTAH	-0.33
4	COLUMBIA	2.27		61	KANSAS	-0.36
5	MICHIGAN	2.26		62	BROWN	-0.37
6	CALIFORNIA, BERKELEY	1.91		63	BOSTON COLLEGE	-0.37
7	NEW YORK	1.81		64	SOUTH CAROLINA	-0.39
8	PENNSYLVANIA STATE	1.40		65	SASKATCHEWAN	-0.39
9	TEXAS	1.34		66	LAVAL	-0.40
10	PRINCETON	1.32		67	CONNECTICUT	-0.40
11	CORNELL	1.32		68	TEMPLE	-0.40
12	CALIFORNIA, LOS ANGELES	1.24		69	MANITOBA	-0.41
13	DUKE	1.23		70	MIT	-0.42
14	OHIO STATE	1.06		71	IOWA STATE	-0.44
15	ILLINOIS, URBANA	0.98		72	KENTUCKY	-0.45
16	SOUTHERN CALIFORNIA	0.96		73	COLORADO	-0.46
17	PENNSYLVANIA	0.90		74	NEW MEXICO	-0.46
18	TEXAS A&M	0.80		75	DARTMOUTH	-0.48
19	WASHINGTON	0.74		76	ROCHESTER	-0.49
20	JOHNS HOPKINS	0.68		77	HOUSTON	-0.50
21	MINNESOTA	0.66		78	CINCINNATI	-0.52
22	BRITISH COLUMBIA	0.65		79	ALABAMA	-0.53
23	EMORY	0.61		80	ILLINOIS, CHICAGO	-0.53
24	RUTGERS	0.58		81	CALIFORNIA, IRVINE	-0.53
25	WISCONSIN	0.54		82	DELAWARE	-0.54
26	ALBERTA	0.52		83	SYRACUSE	-0.54
27	NORTH CAROLINA	0.48		84	SUNY-BUFFALO	-0.56
28	CHICAGO	0.40		85	TULANE	-0.57
29	INDIANA	0.30		86	CALIFORNIA, DAVIS	-0.60
30	NORTHWESTERN	0.29		87	WAYNE STATE	-0.61
31	VIRGINIA	0.22		88	HAWAII	-0.64
32	IOWA	0.18		89	OREGON	-0.64
33	PITTSBURGH	0.16		90	VIRGINIA TECH	-0.67
34	MICHIGAN STATE	0.15		91	FLORIDA STATE	-0.68
35	MCGILL	0.15		92	OKLAHOMA STATE	-0.68
36	MONTREAL	0.15		93	LOUISVILLE	-0.69
37	NORTH CAROLINA STATE	0.07		94	MASSACHUSETTS	-0.70
38	FLORIDA	0.05		95	MISSOURI	-0.70
39	GEORGETOWN	0.03		96	NEBRASKA	-0.71
40	TEXAS TECH	-0.04		97	QUEEN'S	-0.72
41	ARIZONA	-0.05		98	WATERLOO	-0.72
42	CALGARY	-0.08		99	RICE	-0.75
43	MARYLAND	-0.11		100	MCMASTER	-0.77
44	WASHINGTON U.-ST. LOUIS	-0.14		101	CALIFORNIA, SANTA BARBARA	-0.78
45	BRIGHAM YOUNG	-0.14		102	COLORADO STATE	-0.78
46	CALIFORNIA, SAN DIEGO	-0.15		103	GUELPH	-0.85
47	NOTRE DAME	-0.15		104	GEORGIA TECH	-0.87
48	GEORGE WASHINGTON	-0.16		105	CASE WESTERN RESERVE	-0.88
49	TENNESSEE	-0.16		106	SUNY-STONY BROOK	-0.92
50	PURDUE	-0.18		107	LOUISIANA STATE	-0.92
51	MIAMI	-0.20		108	WASHINGTON STATE	-0.95
52	OTTAWA	-0.22		109	SOUTHERN ILLINOIS	-1.00
53	OKLAHOMA	-0.24		110	AUBURN	-1.01
54	YORK	-0.25		111	SUNY-ALBANY	-1.02
55	GEORGIA	-0.28		112	CALIFORNIA, RIVERSIDE	-1.06
56	BOSTON	-0.29		113	OHIO	-1.10
57	VANDERBILT	-0.29		114	KENT STATE	-1.12
				115	HOWARD	-1.13

ARL Statistics Questionnaire 2013–2014

Instructions for Completing the Questionnaire

http://www.arlstatistics.org/

GENERAL OVERVIEW: Definitions of statistical categories can be found in NISO Z39.7-2004, Information Services and Use: Metrics & statistics for libraries and information providers—Data Dictionary (http://www.niso.org/). ARL has augmented some of the language used here to clarify issues of emerging importance to the community based on advice from the ARL Statistics and Assessment Committee (http://www.arl.org/stats/aboutstats/committee).

- Login to submit your data at http://arlstatistics.org/dashboard

- Please do not use decimals. All figures should be rounded to the nearest whole number.

- Please respond to <u>every question</u>. If an exact figure cannot be provided at the data entry form level, leave it blank. The Primary Contact should carefully review the totals for each question; and if they are not representative of the overall institution, the Primary Contact can mark the question NA/UA at the publication level screen. See the Web Data Entry Instructions on the mailing website for further details: http://www.arlstatistics.org/About/Mailings/stats_2013-14.

  Although the form allows for data to be entered from both main and branch campuses, <u>an effort should be made to report figures for the main campus only</u>. (The U.S. National Center for Education Statistics, Integrated Postsecondary Education Data System (IPEDS) defines a branch institution as "a campus or site of an educational institution that is not temporary, is located in a community beyond a reasonable commuting distance from its parent institution, and offers organized programs of study, not just courses"). If figures for libraries located at branch campuses are reported, please specify which branch libraries are included and which ones are excluded in the FOOTNOTES section of the ARL Statistics Worksheet.

- A branch library is defined as an auxiliary library service outlet with quarters separate from the central library of an institution, which has a basic collection of books and other materials, a regular staffing level, and an established schedule. A branch library is administered <u>either</u> by the central library <u>or</u> (as in the case of some law and medical libraries) through the administrative structure of other units within the university. Departmental study/reading rooms are not included.

- The questionnaire assumes a fiscal year ending June 30, 2014. If your fiscal year is different, please indicate this in the FOOTNOTES section of the ARL Statistics Worksheet by adjusting the reporting period.

- Footnotes. Explanatory footnotes will be included with the published statistics. Provide any notes you may have in the footnotes area at the end of the survey. Reporting libraries are urged to record there any information that would clarify the figures submitted in that line, e.g., the inclusion and exclusion of branch campus libraries. Please make an effort to word your footnotes in a manner consistent with notes appearing in the published report, so that the ARL Office can interpret your footnotes correctly. Please use a concise sentence/paragraph format when writing footnotes—do not use "bullets" or make a "bullet list."

ARL libraries are distinguished by the breadth and quality of their collections and services. They are also recognized for their distinctive contributions to the aggregate of research resources in North America, in a variety of media. As such, research library collections are key assets for individual institutions and for the nation. Through individual and cooperative efforts, research libraries strive to preserve the record of knowledge in ARL collections into the future. With the move from print to digital, libraries are providing stewardship not only by the amount of local investments but also by the depth of their collaborations in establishing and supporting shared collections.

The goal of capturing information on content indicators like 'titles' for the purposes of the ARL Statistics annual data collection is tied to the mission of ARL in that it tries to provide good yet practical-to-collect indicators for the rich scholarly resources ARL member libraries make available.

COLLECTIONS:

Question 1. Titles Held. Report all the instances of titles managed and maintained by the library including cataloged, locally digitized, and licensed resources. Counting the 245 field when the library provides stewardship for those resources may be sufficient.

The ANSI/NISO Z39.7-2004 definition for title is as follows:

> The designation of a separate bibliographic whole, whether issued in one or several volumes …. Titles are defined according to the Anglo-American Cataloging Rules. A book or serial title may be distinguished from other such titles by its unique International Standard Book Number (ISBN) or International Standard Serial Number (ISSN). This definition applies equally to print, audiovisual, and other library materials. For unpublished works, the term is used to designate a manuscript collection or an archival record series. Two subscriptions to Science magazine, for example, are counted as one title. When vertical file materials are counted, a file folder is considered a title.

Report the total number of titles catalogued and made ready for use. Consider a title to be the title of a distinct bibliographic manifestation, usually represented by its own bibliographic description or record in the catalog. Count multiple copies of the same manifestation as one title. If the library owns or has access to identical content in different formats, count each format as a different title. For example, a serial title available in print, microform and online would be counted as three titles. Count different editions and versions of the same work as separate titles since they denote depth in the collection.

Do not report here titles for which your library is not providing sustained stewardship and maintenance.

Include special collections materials, government documents, serials and monographs; microforms, computer files, manuscripts and archives, audiovisual materials (cartographic, graphic, audio, film and video, etc.). Special collection materials in particular constitute resources of national/international distinction and the breadth and depth of these resources is a key indicator tied to the mission of research libraries.

Include all materials where financial contribution has been made even if partial.

Include gifts.

If your library digitizes content from its own collection and the content is accessible under current copyright law you can report it. Do not count HathiTrust, CRL, Internet Archive, etc. unless your library owns the digitized item and it is accessible under current copyright law.

For demand driven acquisition report titles only after they are purchased. If a library does not provide access to a title, do not report it.

NOTE: Titles held is not related to the items reported under Volumes held defined prior to 2011–12.

Question 2. Volumes in Library. Use the ANSI/NISO Z39.7-2004 definition for volume as follows:

> a single physical unit of any printed, typewritten, handwritten, mimeographed, or processed work, distinguished from other units by a separate binding, encasement, portfolio, or other clear distinction, which has been cataloged, classified, and made ready for use, and which is typically the unit used to charge circulation transactions. Either a serial volume is bound, or it comprises the serial issues that would be bound together if the library bound all serials.

Include duplicates and bound volumes of periodicals. For purposes of this questionnaire, unclassified bound serials arranged in alphabetical order are considered classified. Exclude microforms, maps, nonprint materials, and uncataloged items. If any of these items cannot be excluded, please provide an explanatory footnote.

Include government document volumes that are accessible through the library's catalogs regardless of whether they are separately shelved. "Classified" includes documents arranged by Superintendent of Documents, CODOC, or similar numbers. "Cataloged" includes documents for which records are provided by the library or downloaded from other sources into the library's card or online catalogs. Documents should, to the extent possible, be counted as they would if they were in bound volumes (e.g., 12 issues of an annual serial would be one or two volumes). Title and piece counts should <u>not</u> be considered the same as volume counts. If a volume count has not been kept, it may be estimated through sampling a representative group of title records and determining the corresponding number of volumes, then extrapolating to the rest of the collection. As an alternative, an estimate may be made using the following formulae:

> 52 documents pieces per foot
>
> 10 "traditional" volumes per foot
>
> 5.2 documents pieces per volume

Include e-book units, as long as these e-books are owned or leased and have been cataloged by your library. Include electronic books purchased through vendors such as NetLibrary® or Books 24x7, and e-books that come as part of aggregate services. Include individual titles of e-book sets that are treated as individual reference sources. Include locally digitized electronic books and electronic theses and dissertations. Provide a footnote reporting the products and the number of titles in a note.

Include volumes purchased collectively where the cost is shared at the time of purchase.

If either formulas or sampling are used for deriving your count, please indicate in a footnote.

Question 3. Basis of Volume Count. A physical count is a piece count; a bibliographic count is a catalog record count.

Question 4. E-books. Report the number of electronic books held. Include electronic theses and dissertations. This number is a subset of Volumes Held reported in Q2.

EXPENDITURES

Questions 6–12. Expenditures. Report all expenditures of funds that come to the library from the regular institutional budget, and from sources such as research grants, special projects, gifts and endowments, and fees for service. (For **Salaries and wages** include non-library funds; see specific instructions below). Do not report encumbrances of funds that have not yet been expended. Canadian libraries should report expenditures in Canadian dollars. (For your information, if interested in determining figures in U.S. dollars, divide Canadian dollar amounts by 1.0706, the average monthly noon exchange rate published in the Bank of Canada Review for the period July 2013–June 2014). Please round figures to the nearest dollar.

Report figures for the following categories of expenditures:

Question 7. Total Library Materials Expenditures.

Question 7a. One time library materials expenditures. Report expenditures for all library materials that are non-subscription, one-time, or monographic in nature; include expenditures for software and machine-readable materials considered part of the collections. Examples include periodical backfiles, literature collections, one-time costs for JSTOR membership, etc.

Question 7b. Ongoing library materials expenditures. Report subscription expenditures (or those which are expected to be ongoing commitments) for serial and other publications; include online searches of remote databases such as OCLC FirstSearch®, DIALOG®, Lexis-Nexis®, etc. Examples include paid subscriptions for print and electronic journals and indexes/abstracts available via the Internet, CD-ROM serials, and annual access fees for resources purchased on a "one-time" basis, such as literature collections, JSTOR membership, etc.

Question 7c. Collection support. Include miscellaneous expenditures as well as document delivery/interlibrary loan. Include materials funds expenditures not included in questions (7a)–(7b), e.g., expenditures for bibliographic utilities, literature searching, security devices, memberships for the purposes of publications, etc. Please list categories, with amounts, in a footnote. Note: If your library does not use materials funds for non-materials expenditures—i.e., if those expenditures are included in "Other Operating Expenditures" — report 0. Include all Contract Binding expenditures—that is only contract expenditures for binding done outside the library. If all binding is done in-house, state this fact and give in-house expenditures in a footnote; do not include personnel expenditures in this question. Some computer hardware and software expenditures may be reported here if they are expended from collection funds.

Question 8. Salaries and wages. Exclude fringe benefits. If professional, support staff and student salaries cannot be separated, check the Manual Override box and enter the total.

Question 8c. Salaries and wages: Student Assistants. Report 100% of student wages regardless of budgetary source of funds. Include federal and local funds for work study students.

Question 9. Other operating expenditures. Exclude expenditures for buildings, maintenance, and fringe benefits. Include computer hardware and software.

Question 10. Fringe Benefits. Include here the dollar amount of fringe benefits. If fringe benefits are not paid

from the library budget please provide an estimate. Use the institution's official designated percent for your estimation. For example, if the library budget for salaries and wages is $2,000,000 and the official designated percent is 30%, multiply $2,000,000*.30 = $600,000 and report the estimated amount of $600,000. As another example, if the official designated percent is 30% for professional staff and 20% for support staff, estimate the dollar amount by multiplying the salaries for professional staff and the salaries for professional staff with the appropriate percent and sum the totals.

Question 11. Official designated percent. Please report here the official designated percent for fringe benefits for the institution. If the official designated percent is 30% for one type of employee and 20% for another type, report here the designated percent for professional library staff. Please provide explanatory footnotes as needed.

Question 12. Consortia/Networks/Bibliographic Utilities Expenditures from External Sources. If the library receives access to computer files, electronic serials or search services through one or more centrally-funded system or consortial arrangements for which it does not pay fully and/or directly (for example, funding is provided by the state on behalf of all members), enter the amount paid by external bodies on its behalf. If the specific dollar amount is not known, but the total student FTE for the consortium and amount spent for the academic members are known, divide the overall amount spent by the institution's share of the total student FTE.

PERSONNEL

Questions 13–13c. Personnel. Report the number of FTE (full-time equivalent) staff in filled positions, or positions that are only temporarily vacant. ARL defines temporarily vacant positions as positions that were vacated during the fiscal year for which ARL data were submitted, for which there is a firm intent to refill, and for which there are expenditures for salaries reported in the *Expenditures* section.

Include cost recovery positions and staff hired for special projects and grants, but provide an explanatory footnote indicating the number of such staff. If such staff cannot be included, provide a footnote. To compute full-time equivalents of part-time employees and student assistants, take the total number of hours per week (or year) worked by part-time employees in each category and divide it by the number of hours considered by the reporting library to be a full-time work week (or year). Round figures to the nearest whole numbers.

Exclude maintenance and custodial staff.

Report figures for the following groups of personnel:

Question 13a. Professional Staff. Since the criteria for determining professional status vary among libraries, there is no attempt to define the term "professional." Each library should report those staff members it considers professional, including, when appropriate, staff who are not librarians in the strict sense of the term, for example computer experts, systems analysts, or budget officers.

Question 13b. Support Staff. Report the total FTE (see *Personnel*, above) of staff are not included in *Professional Staff*.

Question 13c. Student Assistants. Report the total FTE (see *Personnel*, above) of student assistants employed on an hourly basis whose wages are paid from funds under library control <u>or from a budget other</u> than the library's, including federal work-study programs.

INSTRUCTION

Questions 14–15. Instruction. <u>Sampling based on a typical week may be used to extrapolate TO A FULL YEAR.</u> Please indicate if responses are based on sampling.

Report figures for the following:

Question 14. Presentations to Groups. Report the total number of sessions during the year of presentations made as part of formal bibliographic instruction programs and through other planned class presentations, orientation sessions, and tours. If the library sponsors multi-session or credit courses that meet several times over the course of a semester, each session should be counted. Presentations to groups may be for either bibliographic instruction, cultural, recreational, or educational purposes. Presentations both on and off the premises should be included as long as they are sponsored by the library. Do not include meetings sponsored by other groups using library meeting rooms. Do not include training for library staff; the purpose of this question is to capture information about the services the library provides for its clientele. Please indicate if the figure is based on sampling.

Question 15. Participants in Group Presentations. Report the total number of attendees in all group presentations (as defined in *Presentations to Groups,* above). For multi-session classes with a constant enrollment, count each person only once. Please indicate if the figure is based on sampling. Use a footnote to describe any special situations.

NOTE: Personal, one-to-one instruction in the use of sources should be counted as reference transactions as described in the next section.

REFERENCE

Question 16. Reference Transactions. Report the total number of reference transactions.

A reference transaction is

> an information contact that involves the *knowledge, use, recommendations, interpretation, or instruction in the use* [or creation *of*] *one or more information sources* by a member of the library staff. The term includes information and referral service. Information sources include (a) printed and nonprinted materials; (b) machine-readable databases (including computer-assisted instruction); (c) the library's own catalogs and other holdings records; (d) other libraries and institutions through communication or referral; and (e) persons both inside and outside the library. When a staff member uses information gained from previous use of information sources to answer a question, the [transaction] is reported as a [reference transaction] even if the source is not consulted again. *[Note: this is a modified ANSI/NISO Z39.7-2004 definition for an information request]*

If a contact includes both reference and directional services, it should be reported as one reference transaction. Include virtual reference transactions (e.g., e-mail, WWW form, chat). Duration should not be an element in determining whether a transaction is a reference transaction. <u>Sampling based on a typical week may be used to extrapolate TO A FULL YEAR.</u> Please indicate if the figure is based on sampling.

EXCLUDE SIMPLE DIRECTIONAL QUESTIONS. A directional transaction is an information contact that facilitates the logistical use of the library and that does not involve the knowledge, use, recommendations, interpretation, or instruction in the use or creation of information sources other than those that describe the library, such as schedules, floor plans, and handbooks.

CIRCULATION

Question 17. Initial circulations (excluding reserves). Count the number of initial circulations during the fiscal year from the general collection for use usually (although not always) outside the library. <u>Do not count renewals.</u> Include circulations to and from remote storage facilities for library users (i.e., do <u>not</u> include transactions reflecting transfers or stages of technical processing). Count the total number of items lent, not the number of borrowers.

USE OF ELECTRONIC RESOURCES

Questions 18–20. Use of Electronic Resources. Items reported should follow definitions as defined in the COUNTER Code of Practice (www.projectcounter.org). In a footnote, please include the types of resources for which you are reporting data. It is recommend that ONLY data that follow the COUNTER definitions be reported. Any exceptions should be documented in a footnote.

INTERLIBRARY LOANS

Questions 21–22. Interlibrary Loans. Report **the number of requests for material** (both returnables and non-returnables) **provided to other libraries** and **the number of filled requests received from other libraries or providers.** For both of these figures, include originals, photocopies, and materials sent by fax or other forms of electronic transmission. Include patron-initiated transactions. Exclude requests for materials locally owned and available on the shelves or electronically. Do not include transactions between libraries covered by this questionnaire.

UNIVERSITY CHARACTERISTICS: Doctor's Degrees, Faculty, Enrollment

Question 23. Doctor's Degrees. Report the number awarded during the 2013–14 fiscal year. For the purposes of this report, Doctor's degrees include research/scholarship degrees and professional practice degrees (e.g., Ph.D, D.Ed., D.P.A., M.D., J.D., etc.) as enumerated in the U.S. Department of Education's Integrated Postsecondary Education Data System (IPEDS). Any exceptions should be footnoted.

Question 24. Doctor's Degrees Fields. For the purposes of this report, Doctor's degrees fields are defined as the specific discipline specialties enumerated in the U.S. Department of Education's Integrated Postsecondary Education Data System (IPEDS) "Completions" Survey. Any exceptions should be footnoted.

Question 25. Instructional Faculty. Instructional faculty are defined by the U.S. Dept. of Education as:

> members of the instruction/research staff who are employed full-time as defined by the institution, including faculty with released time for research and faculty on sabbatical leave.

Full-time counts generally <u>exclude</u> faculty who are employed to teach fewer than two semesters, three quarters, two trimesters, or two four-month sessions; replacements for faculty on sabbatical leave or leave without pay; faculty for preclinical and clinical medicine; faculty who are donating their services; faculty who are members of military organizations and paid on a different pay scale from civilian employees; academic officers, whose primary duties are administrative; and graduate students who assist in the instruction of courses. Please be sure the number reported, and the basis for counting, are consistent with those for 2012–13 (unless in previous years faculty were counted who should have been excluded according to the above definition). Please footnote any discrepancies.

Questions 26–29. Enrollment. U.S. libraries should use the Fall 2013 enrollment figures reported to the Department of Education on the Integrated Postsecondary Education Data System survey. Please check these figures against the enrollment figures reported to ARL last year to ensure consistency and accuracy. NOTE: In the past, the number of part-time students reported was FTE; the number now reported to IPEDS is a head count of part-time students. Canadian libraries should note that the category "graduate students" as reported here includes all post-baccalaureate students.

FOOTNOTES

Please consult the data entry Web interface (www.arlstatistics.org) for a copy of last year's footnotes. These can be found under "Data Repository" after you login into www.arlstatistics.org. Explanatory footnotes will be included with the published statistics. Reporting libraries are urged to record in the footnote section any information that would clarify the figures submitted, e.g., the inclusion and exclusion of branch campus libraries (see the "General Instructions" for definition of branch campus libraries). Please make an effort to word your footnotes in a manner consistent with notes appearing in the published report, so that the ARL office can interpret your footnotes correctly.

NOTE: Any large shifts in reported data compared to last year should be explained with a footnote.

Submit the completed questionnaire
By October 15, 2014

For assistance, please e-mail or Google chat: stats@arl.org
Tel. (202) 296-2296; FAX (202) 872-0884

ARL Statistics 2013–2014 Worksheet

This worksheet is designed to help you plan your submission for the 2013–2014 *ARL Statistics*. The figures on this worksheet should be similar to those in the "Summary" page of your web form, except in cases where data are unavailable. If an exact figure is unavailable, leave it blank. The Primary Contact should carefully review the totals for each question; and if they are not representative of the overall institution, the Primary Contact can mark the question NA/UA at the publication level screen.

Reporting Institution _____ Date Returned to ARL _____

Report Prepared by (name) _____

Title _____

Email address _____ Phone number _____

Contact person (if different) _____

Title _____

Email address _____ Phone number _____

COLLECTIONS:

1. **Titles held June 30, 2014 (all formats)**   (1) _____

2. **Volumes held June 30, 2014 (print plus electronic)**   (2) _____

3. **Basis of print volume count is**   (3) _____Physical

                                 _____Bibliographic

4. **Electronic books (included in question 2)**   (4) _____

5. **Are the below figures reported in Canadian dollars?**   (5) _____Yes _____No

EXPENDITURES

6. **Total Library Expenditures (exclude fringe benefits)** *(7 + 8 + 9)*   (6) _____

7. **Total Library Materials Expenditures** *(7a + 7b + 7c)*   (7) _____

   7a. One-time resource purchases   (7a) _____

   7b. Ongoing resource purchases

      (e.g., subscriptions, annual license fees)   (7b) _____

   7c. Collection support   (7c) _____

8. **Total Salaries and Wages** *(8a + 8b + 8c)*

    (Exclude fringe benefits; **Report fringe benefits in question 10**)   **(8)**_____

    8a. Professional staff (exclude fringe benefits)   (8a)_____

    8b. Support staff (exclude fringe benefits)   (8b)_____

    8c. Student assistants (exclude fringe benefits)   (8c)_____

9. **Other operating expenditures**   **(9)**_____

FRINGE BENEFITS (Provide a detailed footnote on what this includes)

10. **Fringe benefits**   **(10)**_____

11. **Official designated percent**   **(11)**_____

EXPENDITURES FROM EXTERNAL SOURCES

12. **Consortia/Networks/Bibliographic Utilities Expenditures**

    from External Sources   **(12)**_____

PERSONNEL (Round figures to nearest whole number)

13. **Total Staff FTE** *(13a + 13b + 13c)*   **(13)**_____

    13a. Professional staff, FTE   (13a)_____

    13b. Support staff, FTE   (13b)_____

    13c. Student assistants, FTE   (13c)_____

INSTRUCTION

14. **Number of library presentations to groups**   **(14)**_____

    14a. Is the library presentations figure based on sampling?   (14a)_____Yes   _____No

15. **Number of total participants in group presentations reported**

    in line 14   **(15)**_____

    15a. Is the total participants in group presentations figure based on sampling?

    (15a)_____Yes   _____No

REFERENCE

16. **Number of reference transactions**   **(16)**_____

    16a. Is the reference transactions figure based on sampling?   (16a)_____Yes   _____No

CIRCULATION

17. Number of initial circulations (excluding reserves) (17)_____

USE OF ELECTRONIC RESOURCES (following COUNTER definitions)

18. Number of successful full-text article requests (journals) (18)_____

19. Number of regular searches (databases) (19)_____

20. Number of federated searches (databases) (20)_____

INTERLIBRARY LOANS

21. Total number of filled requests <u>provided</u> to other libraries (21)_____

22. Total number of filled requests <u>received</u> from other libraries or

     providers (22)_____

DOCTOR'S DEGREES AND FACULTY

23. Number of Doctor's Degrees awarded in FY2013–2014 (23)_____

24. Number of fields in which Doctor's Degrees can be awarded (24)_____

25. Number of full-time instructional faculty in FY2013–2014 (25)_____

ENROLLMENT – FALL 2013

26. Full-time students, undergraduate and graduate (26)_____

27. Part-time students, undergraduate and graduate (27)_____

28. Full-time graduate students (28)_____

29. Part-time graduate students (29)_____

FOOTNOTES

NOTE: Any large shifts in reported data compared to last year should be explained with a footnote.

Submit the completed questionnaire
By October 15, 2014

For assistance, please e-mail or Google chat: stats@arl.org
Tel. (202) 296-2296; FAX (202) 872-0884

THIS PAGE INTENTIONALLY LEFT BLANK

FOOTNOTES

Footnotes may also include errata and corrections to data from prior years not previously reported. Numbers refer to columns in Library Data Tables and to Questionnaire numbers. Unless otherwise stated all figures are as of 06/30/2014.

QUESTION NUMBER	FOOTNOTE

ALABAMA

	All figures are as of 09/30/2014.
	Library branches included: Amelia Gayle Gorgas, Bruno Business Library, McLure Education Library, Rodgers Library for Science & Engineering, Hoole Special Collections.
2	Bibliographic information has been updated in the past year.
7.a	We did not purchase as many one-time resources in 2013–2014.
16	Increase in outreach and accuracy in documenting reference transactions.

ALBERTA

	All figures are as of 03/31/2014.
	Library branches included: Augustana Campus Library, Book and Record Depository (BARD), Bibliotheque Saint Jean, Bruce Peel Special Collections Library, Cameron (Science and Technology) Library, Data Library, Herbert T. Coutts (Education and Physical Education) Library, Rutherford (Humanities and Social Sciences) Library, John A. Weir Memorial Law Library, John W. Scott Health Sciences Library, Winspear Business Reference Library, and University of Alberta Archives.
6–9, 10, 12	Expenditures as reported in Canadian dollars. Collections Expenditures: (7a) $6,701,992; (7b) $12,803,555; (7c) $1,632,051; (7) $21,137,598; Salary Expenditures: (8a) $7,810,256; (8b) $7,458,568; (8c) $671,812; (8) $15,940,636; (10) $3,522,661; Overall Expenditures: (7) $21,137,598; (8) $15,940,636; (9) $3,782,901; (6) $40,861,135; (12) NA/UA. NOTE: Total Salaries and Wages (Q8) EXCLUDES Fringe Benefits Expenditures (Q10).
7.c	Effective 2013–2014, collection support figure includes cataloguing and shelf-ready processing.
10	Figure for fringe benefits includes long term disability, employment insurance, Canada Pension Plan, Alberta Workers Compensation Board contributions, University Pension Plan, dental plan, supplementary health coverage, life insurance, Employee and Family Assistance Program, critical illness insurance, and Public Services Pension Plan contributions.
20	Significant increase in number of federated searches due to increased use of discovery layer search interface.

ARIZONA

	Library branches included: Science and Engineering, Fine Arts.

ARIZONA STATE

	Library branches included: Added a new campus called ASU Lake Havasu.
4	Includes addition of over 136K e-book MARC records loaded FY 2014, including large record loads of 36K for new purchase of Early American Imprints Series I–II; and 44K for updated Ebrary Academic Complete and NCCO Parts I–VIII packages. E-book records newly loaded FY 2014 for Making of Modern Law, LoisLaw, and Hein Online packages.
7.a	Decrease largely due to $137K reduction in operations transfers to materials budget FY 2014, and deduction of $167K in FY14 for payments from deposit account established in FY 2011, FY 2012, and FY 2013 included $125K each for major manuscript collection purchase, completed in two payments so not paid FY 2014.

Question Number	Footnote

ARIZONA STATE cont.

7.c	Includes DocDel/ILL $35,640; Contract binding $119,753; Conservation/Preservation $27,480; Memberships $124,006; Staff use software $35,893; MARC records $975; Digitization $40,390 Digitization of IsraPulp special collection. Purchased MARC records for any new and some existing electronic databases from an outside vendor.
9	Transfers of $500,000 to new local account; & $586,552 to materials budget. Installed new flooring and had some chutes built for the weeding project. Also purchased video equipment and new workstations.
10	Fringe benefits include: medical, retirement, and insurance.
13.c	When reporting financials, ASU no longer reports student FTE.
14	Fewer requests for presentations.
16	Possible under-reporting of our virtual reference statistics in previous years.
17	Perhaps because of increased use of e-books.
18	A higher percentage of journals were accessed.
20	Shows an increase in simultaneous search of multiple searchable resources.

AUBURN

	All figures are as of 09/30/2014.
	Library branches included: Library of Architecture, Design and Construction; and Charles Cary Veterinary Medical Library.
7.a	The decrease is due to last year's one-time purchase of a Civil War collection for $100,000.
7.c	Decrease in bindery.
10	Includes on-the-job injury, FICA, unemployment, mandatory retirement, voluntary retirement matching, retiree insurance (PEEHIP), life insurance, long-term disability, health insurance, employee tuition reimbursement, termination payments, and professional leave payments.
14	One course eliminated its library instruction sessions.
16	The higher number of reference transactions may be due to an improved online interface for recording questions and greater diligence during the sampling week.
19	Additional databases are now COUNTER compliant.
28	The definitions of FT and PT graduate student were changed.

BOSTON

	Library branches included: Theology (included in Main), Gotlieb Archival Research Center (Special Collections) (included in Main), Law and Health Sciences.
2	Mugar had a 4.6% increase in volume count in FY 2014 as compared with the previous FY. This increase is mostly due to our improving the accuracy of our e-book holdings.
7.c	Categories included in Q7c are: OCLC First Search ($25,192), Contract Binding ($66,366), In-house Binding ($4,363), ILL Delivery ($18,975), and Memberships ($75,123).
17	Number of initial circulations excluding reserves of print books decreased by 41% in FY 2014 as compared with the previous FY. Our patrons are tending to use e-books more frequently than print books. We have an e-preferred acquisitions policy in place so more and more of our book acquisitions are electronic.
18, 20	Counts reported for this question on the main library survey are for all Boston University libraries.

QUESTION NUMBER	FOOTNOTE

BOSTON cont.

19 — Relevant COUNTER reports have been gathered from as many publishers and platforms as possible, reporting use of journal frontlists, backfiles and archives, and aggregated databases and indexes.

BOSTON COLLEGE

All figures are as of 05/31/2014.

Library branches included: Bapst Library, Burns Library, Educational Resource Center, Social Work Library, Theology and Ministry Library.

1 — Title count includes the BC Law Library as well as all branch libraries.

10 — Includes tuition remission, life insurance, long-term disability insurance, TIAA-CREF and Fidelity retirement plans, medical insurance, dental insurance, adoption benefit, sick leave, vacation time, and paid holidays.

11 — Editor's Note: Published figure reflects the official designated percent for the Law Library, as this is the maximum value entered for this question.

12 — List price of databases provided to us by the State of MA.

16.a — Both the Social Work Library and the Educational Resource Center indicated that their figures were based on sampling, while O'Neill, Theology and Ministry, Bapst, and Burns Libraries were not based on sampling.

19 — Many more platforms added DB1 Reports in 2014.

20 — Service was not promoted this year, and is not easily identified on the website.

23 — Includes law degrees awarded.

25 — Report for 2012–2013 mistakenly counted law faculty twice. The correct figure was 761, not 814.

26–28 — Includes law students.

29 — No information provided regarding the decline in part-time graduate students.

BRIGHAM YOUNG

All figures are as of 12/31/2013.

4 — Several thousand e-book records were accidentally loaded into our catalog twice. We corrected this error which makes it appear that our e-book numbers went down over the past year when, in fact, they increased slightly.

7.c — Last year's figure for this item inadvertently omitted Document Delivery/Interlibrary Loan. This should have resulted in a figure of 265,766 for the Main Library, and when added to the Law figure of the same, which was 8,426, would give a total for the ARL Publication of 274,192. Hence the change from last year to this year would have been only 9%.

11 — Editor's Note: Published figure reflects the official designated percent for the Law Library, as this is the maximum value entered for this question.

18, 19 — BYU added two significant databases of full-text journals in 2013, as well as obtained stats from some databases that did not previously report them.

20 — BYU integrated the EBSCO API into BYU's discovery tool, which uses federated searching to return results.

BRITISH COLUMBIA

All figures are as of 03/31/2014.

BRITISH COLUMBIA cont.

	Library branches included: Asian Library, Biomedical Branch Library, David Lam Library, Dr. John Micallef Memorial Library (St. Mark's College), Education Library, H.R. MacMillan Library (Vancouver School of Theology), John Richard Allison Library (Regent College), Music, Art and Architecture Library, Okanagan Library, Rare-books & Special Collections, Robson Square Library, University Archives, Woodward Library, and Xwi7xwa Library (First Nations House of Learning).
	Data from the law and health sciences libraries are included in the figures reported.
1	Increase over previous year because 2012–2013 did not include online titles.
4	Includes catalogued OA and free content accessible through library search interfaces.
6–9, 10, 12	Expenditures as reported in Canadian dollars. Collections Expenditures: (7a) $4,815,656; (7b) $12,978,129; (7c) $152,818; (7) $17,946,603; Salary Expenditures: (8a) $11,103,083; (8b) $6,496,305; (8c) $1,379,847; (8) $18,979,235; (10) $3,466,183; Overall Expenditures: (7) $17,946,603; (8) $18,979,235; (9) $6,994,772; (6) $43,920,610; (12) NA/UA. NOTE: Total Salaries and Wages (Q8) EXCLUDES Fringe Benefits Expenditures (Q10).
6	Increase reflects investment in Centre for Scholarly Communication (Okanagan campus), higher GPOF collections expenditures, and value of donated collections.
7	Increase due to higher GPOF collections expenditures and the value of donated collections.
7.a	Includes collections gifts in kind valued at 1.7M.
7.c	Significantly lower binding and ILL costs.
9	Includes 1.3M for Centre for Scholarly Communications.
10	Includes fringe benefits for professional staff, support staff, and student assistants.
11	Designated percent for professional library staff only.
14, 15	Decrease reflects shift to online delivery of some instructional material.
16	Consolidation and closure of service points contributed to decline in reference transactions.

BROWN

	Library branches included: Rockefeller Library, Sciences Library (which includes the Medical Library), John Hay Library, Orwig Music Library, Library Collections Annex, John Carter Brown Library. Medical library statistics cannot be disaggregated from the main because the medical collection is an integral part of the Sciences Library.
1, 2, 4	Includes large e-book collection added.
8.c	Decrease reflects fewer graduate students (with monthly stipends), as well as the transfer away from Brown of the Women's Writers Project and their funded students.
16	John Hay Library closed for renovation during FY 2014. Also, aberration in the recording of reference statistics.
20	Reflects continued changes in search behavior since introduction of discovery search tool; materials now indexed in the discovery tool and fewer federated searches performed.
23, 27, 29	Annual fluctuations.

CALGARY

	All figures are as of 03/31/2014.
	Library branches included: Taylor Family Digital Library; Health Sciences Library; Bennett Jones Law Library; Business Library; Doucette Library of Teaching Resources; Gallagher Library; Downtown Campus Library; The Military Museums Library and Archives; and the University of Calgary in Qatar–Learning Commons.

QUESTION NUMBER	FOOTNOTE

CALGARY cont.

4 — Increase primarily as the result of the number of e-books purchased through vendors, as well as the number of e-books that come as part of aggregate services.

6–9, 10, 12 — Expenditures as reported in Canadian dollars. Collections Expenditures: (7a) $2,391,437; (7b) $9,323,346; (7c) $1,282,858; (7) $12,997,641; Salary Expenditures: (8a) $6,853,204; (8b) $8,963,174; (8c) $635,683; (8) $16,452,061; (10) $3,539,677; Overall Expenditures: (7) $12,997,641; (8) $16,452,061; (9) $1,368,080; (6) $30,817,782; (12) $299,455. NOTE: Total Salaries and Wages (Q8) EXCLUDES Fringe Benefits Expenditures (Q10).

7.c — Includes document delivery, binding, software, metadata, shelf-ready processing, open access publishing, memberships, evaluations, digitization charges, shipping; decrease in collection support in 2013–2014 as a result of having paid for two years of software support in 2012–2013.

10 — Fringe benefits include: extended health care, dental, accidental death and dismemberment, pension, wellness spending, tuition support, and professional expense reimbursement.

11 — The designated percentage for benefits varies by staff category: 20% for academic staff, 22% for other professional staff, and 24.5% for support staff.

14, 15 — Decrease reflects a change in how librarians interact with users: fewer formal sessions scheduled, more one-on-one support, and more technology-related instruction.

19 — Decrease in regular searches (databases) results from users preferring to use the single search box on the library website to search databases, rather than use the native interface of some databases.

20 — This category within ScholarlyStats does not include usage of Summon, our unified discovery service, which we would include in the category of federated searches; total searches from Summon for the same time period is 1,407,549.

22 — Will monitor over the next reporting year to see whether this increase reflects an upward trend in the number of interlibrary loan requests received from other libraries and to confirm that statistics reporting is handled consistently across the system.

23 — D.Ed. degrees added.

29 — Decrease in the number of part-time graduate students is related to the restructuring of the graduate programs in the Faculty of Education.

CALIFORNIA, BERKELEY

— Library branches included: Anthropology, Art History/Classics, Bancroft, Bioscience & Natural Resources, Business, Chemistry/Chemical Engineering, Data Lab, Doe, Earth Sciences/Maps, East Asian, Education/Psychology, Engineering, Environmental Design, Graduate Services, Mathematics/Statistics, Media Resources Center, Moffitt, Morrison, Music, Newspapers/Microforms, Optometry/Health Sciences, Northern Regional Library Facility, Physics/Astronomy, Public Health, Social Welfare, South/Southeast Asia. The affiliated libraries are not branches of the main library, but their data is included in this publication.

7.a — Included the library and special collections: 5,065,911 + 1,630,463.

9 — Fringe benefits are also included in this category. They weren't included last year.

11 — We have a 3-tiered rate system for assessing fringe benefit expenses. For FY 2013–2014 the percentages of salary were: Academic 33.9%, Staff 41.5%, and Limited (temp) 17.3%. Students are not assessed for fringe benefits.

CALIFORNIA, DAVIS

— Library branches included: Main Library = Shields Library and Physical Sciences & Engineering Library.

7.c — Collection Support Expenditures are included with Other Operating Expenditures.

CALIFORNIA, DAVIS cont.

13.b   Support staffing levels have been reduced due to retirements and other departures. Staffing plans being evaluated during reorganization efforts.

CALIFORNIA, IRVINE

Library branches included: Health Sciences Library and Law Library.

CALIFORNIA, LOS ANGELES

4   Demand by patrons and DDA programs increased our e-book share for 2013/2014.

7.b   Increase in the cost of ongoing resources over 2012–13 was driven by price increases in electronic serials.

10, 11   UCLA does not use official employee benefit rates for recording employee benefit expenditures. UCLA employee benefit expenditures are recorded by the UCLA payroll system at the individual employee level based on each employee's eligibility for benefits and other criteria that may impact the cost of one or more components of employee benefit expense. Year-to-year increase in employee benefit expenditures is driven principally by the UC Regents mandated increase in the employer contributions to the UC retirement plan.

20   Each year usage data collection improves for us and we are able to offer more specific data.

CALIFORNIA, RIVERSIDE

4   This figure includes 124,675 e-books that were omitted from last year's data.

10   This figure includes the following: Employer contributions to OASDI, Medicare, workers compensation insurance, employee support program, unemployment insurance, UC retirement plan, vacation, assessment, staff recognition program, other post employment benefit, health insurance, life insurance, UC paid disability, dental and vision plan premiums, senior management supplement, etc.

CALIFORNIA, SAN DIEGO

Library branches included: Geisel Library, Biomedical Library Building, SIO Collection, and Annex.

4   Improved funding and opportunities allowed increased purchases of e-books, answering a trend of increased demand for digital media.

7.a   Improved budget/funding after a period of restrained allocations.

8.c, 13.c   Improved budget/funding after a period of restrained allocations to student assistants, and program directors in new roles began filling out their new department staffing.

10   Fringe benefits costs include: variable costs fixed costs, annuitant health/dental program (including admin) dental plan, employee incentive award program, health plan, employee support program, life insurance (employee paid), Medicare, non-industrial disability insurance, OASDI vision plan, UC retirement plan, unemployment insurance, and workers' compensation insurance.

12   For all UC libraries: Proportion of expenditures (campus and CDL co-invest portion)–SCAP expenditures = $1,439,798; CDL expenditures continuing = $4,212,604; CDL expenditures one-time = $1,693,188; TOTAL = $7,345,590. NOTE: Does not include memberships, scholarly communication expenses, or expenses for shared-print.

14   Down over the past year because program directors in new roles began their new department commitments: outreach is expected to increase again in the new FY.

15   Down because the number of instruction and outreach offerings decreased this year.

16   This number was down over last year: Suspected that there was some double-counting last year, and this year reference transactions were consolidated across the library and reporting unified. We expect stability over the next FY.

CALIFORNIA, SAN DIEGO cont.

17	Consistent with a reduction in the use of physical resources over electronic resources, and a commensurate decline in library gate.
18, 20	Exact number not available.
22	Interlibrary Loan participation has been declining as use of electronic library resources has increased.
23	494 PhDs and 130 MDs. The lower number may reflect PhD demographics or economic factors.
25	Better budget and endowments have allowed for increased hiring after a period of reductions.
27, 29	The higher number may reflect student demographics or economic factors.

CALIFORNIA, SANTA BARBARA

	Library branches included: Arts Library.
1	Improved count of items, including non-print resources.
2	Improved count of items kept in remote storage.
10	Medical and retirement.
13	Significant turn-over [ca. 30%] during this fiscal year.
17	Construction during last year has been disruptive and gate counts along with circulation counts have gone down.
18	Perhaps reflective of electronic-preferred collection development strategy.
19, 20	Cannot provide an accurate number at this time.

CASE WESTERN RESERVE

	Library branches included: Harris Library at the Mandel School of Applied Social Sciences.
7.c	Includes Bindery, ILL and memberships for CRL, SPARC, ARL, and CNI.
18	Includes: ACM Digital Library, AAAS Science Online Package, AGU Digital Library, American Economic Association Journals, American Chemical Society Journals, American Physical Society Journals, Annual Reviews, ASCE, ASME, APA-PsycArticles, Cambridge University Press Journals, EBSCOhost, Elsevier Science Direct, Gale Cengage, IEEE Xplore Digital Library, Ingenta, Institute of Physics, JAMA, JSTOR, Lexis Nexis, Nature Online, Optical Society of America, Oxford Journals, Project Muse, Project Euclid, ProQuest, Royal Society of Chemistry, Taylor & Francis Journals, and Web of Knowledge.

CHICAGO

	Library branches included: All University of Chicago libraries included.
4	Numbers for 2011–2012 and 2012–2013 incorrectly included e-books from the HathiTrust. The correct number for 2011–2012 was 1,251,085, and the correct number for 2012–2013 was 1,308,057.
7.c	Includes contract binding, vendor-supplied cataloging, table of contents services, etc.
14, 15	We scaled back our tour program this year, so didn't offer as many tours of our Joe and Rika Mansueto Library.
19	The number reported last year was for federated searches (databases) rather than for regular searches (databases). The correct number for last year was 32,915,130.
20	The number reported last year was for regular searches (databases) rather than for federated searches (databases). The correct number for last year was 5,069,304.
21	Increase is due to joining the Borrow Direct consortial borrowing service with the Ivy Plus libraries.
26, 28	Enrollment figures based on the Wednesday of the 4th week of Autumn Quarter.

QUESTION NUMBER	FOOTNOTE

CHICAGO cont.

27   Enrollment figures based on the Wednesday of the 4th week of Autumn Quarter. Decrease from last year due to declines in part-time graduate population due to year-to-year variability in this category of student.

29   Enrollment figures based on the Wednesday of the 4th week of Autumn Quarter. Decrease from last year due to year-to-year variability in this category of student.

CINCINNATI

Library branches included: Overall survey statistics include all University of Cincinnati Libraries, including the main library, health sciences library, law library, eight college and departmental libraries (Archives and Rare-books; Chemistry-Biology; Classics; Design, Architecture, Art and Planning; Education, Criminal Justice and Human Services; Engineering and Applied Science; Geology-Mathematics-Physics; and Music), and two regional campus libraries (Clermont College and Blue Ash College).

4   FY 2013–2014 e-books included in Collections/Packages:
113 20th century African American poetry (Online). OCU
731 20th century American poetry (Online). OCU
585 20th century English poetry (Online). OCU
657 ABC-Clio E-Books. OCU
3768 ACLS History E-Books. OCU
1222 ACS Symposium Series. OCU
194 African writers series (Online). OCU
100 African-American Poetry 1760–1900 (Online). OCU
706 American drama (Online). OCU
1288 American Poetry 1600–1900. OCU
3822 APA PsychBOOKS. OCU
16131 Chadwyck-Healey Literature online. OCU
7188 CRCnetBASE. OCU
681 Credo reference. OCU
1226 Directory of open access books. OCU
565 Early American fiction, 1774–1850 (Online). OCU
37370 Early American imprints (Online). First series, Evans. OCU
38093 Early American imprints (Online). Second series, Shaw-Shoemaker. OCU
94072 Early English books online
145 Editions and adaptations of Shakespeare (Online). OCU
184092 Eighteenth century collections online
96 Eighteenth century fiction (Online). OCU
729 Emerald business, management and economics ebook series. OCU
1826 Engineering Village 2. OCU
4469 English poetry database (Online)
1653 English prose drama (Online)
2283 English verse drama (Online). OCU
122 Gale virtual reference library (Online). OCU
300 Geological Society special publication. OCU
1482 HeinOnline Legal Classics collection. OCU
421 IEEE Xplore digital library. OCU
290 IET digital library. IET e-books. OCU
1763 IGI Global Research Collection. OCU
2622 Knovel library. OCU
111125 LexisNexis U.S. Congressional Hearings Digital Collection
358214 LexisNexis U.S. serial set digital collection
7480 Making of America (University of Michigan)
21791 Making of modern law (Online)

QUESTION NUMBER	FOOTNOTE

CINCINNATI cont.

4 cont.

63420 Making of the modern world (Online). OCU
15 Momentum Press e-books. OCU
20460 NBER working paper series online. OCU
11927 NetLibrary E-Books
13337 Nineteenth Century collections online. OCU
11518 OECD iLibrary. Books. OCU
35 Oxford reference. OCU
5618 Oxford scholarship online. OCU
9355 ProQuest Dissertations & Theses
44361 Sabin Americana, 1500–1926
23117 Safari books online. OCU
118 Sage eReference. OCU
1085 ScienceDirect eBook Series. OCU
7 SOLR (Sharpe online reference). OCU
167 SPIE digital library. SPIE e-books. OCU
36967 Springer e-books. OCU
2914 University of Adelaide Library e-books. OCU
21 W.B. Yeats collection (Online). OCU
3046 Wiley InterScience e-books. OCU
1169 Women and social movements in the United States 1600–2000. OCU
8200 World Bank e-book. OCU

8.b — Expenditures for support staff declined due to a shift of staffing from support staff to professional staff.

9 — The total expenditures for Other Operating Expenses decreased compared to last year as funds were encumbered during the year, but not yet expended, for planned internal renovations and improvements.

11 — Fringe benefits rates are dependent upon staff category according to the following: Faculty 41.1%; Staff 33.2%.

18 — With greater use of our discovery service from our main site, the number of successful full-text article requests decreased. This is likely due to more efficient searching with better search results.

COLORADO

Library branches included: Main; Music; Engineering, Mathematics, & Physics; Earth Science & Map; and Business.

4 — Changes to approval plan to acquire more e-books and additional e-book databases.

10 — Calculated based on campus rates for salary categories.

12 — Reduction of subsidy from consortium.

18 — JR1 reports.

19 — DR1 and PR1 reports. Increase due to changes in COUNTER reports.

20 — DR1 and PR1 reports. Decrease due to 5.8 million fewer federated searches on EBSCO platform.

COLORADO STATE

1, 2, 4 — Difference due to a new internal department calculating data.

8.a, 8.b, 13.a, 13.b — State of Colorado permits some staff classifications to be moved to professional depending upon job duties. This is why this number increased.

COLUMBIA

All figures are as of 8/31/2014. [Teachers College]

QUESTION NUMBER	FOOTNOTE

COLUMBIA cont.

	Columbia data includes The Columbia Center for New Media Teaching and Learning (CCNMTL) and the Center for Digital Research and Scholarship (CDRS). [Butler]
1	Excludes HathiTrust titles. [Butler]
11	Official designated percent for Teachers College is 34.7%; 33.7% is shown here in order to reflect a truer representation of the overall Columbia fringe benefits rate. [Teachers College]
18	Downloads from the Children's Literature Comprehensive Database (CLCD) were missing and estimated. [Teachers College]
19	Number changes of regular and federated searches are due to a change in discovery platform. [Teachers College]
21, 22	Excludes ILL for Barnard handled by Butler office. [Barnard]

CONNECTICUT

	Library branches included: Avery Point, Stamford, Torrington, Waterbury, and West Hartford regional campus libraries. Branch libraries also include the Music and Dramatic Arts Library, the Pharmacy Library, and the University Archives and Special Collections at the main campus (Storrs).
10	Fringe benefits include pension, unemployment compensation, health services, group life insurance, social security, and medical insurance.

CORNELL

	Library branches included: All libraries and special collections on the Ithaca, New York City, and Geneva NY campuses: Adelson (ornithology), Africana, Annex (remote storage facility), Asia Collections, Engineering (virtual library), Fine Arts, Hospitality/Labor/Management, Law, Mann (agricultural & life sciences), Mathematics, Music, Olin/Uris (humanities & social sciences), Physical Sciences (virtual library), Rare & Manuscript Collections, and Veterinary Libraries in Ithaca; Medical Library and Medical Center Archives in New York City; and New York Agricultural Experiment Station Library in Geneva NY.
	Library branches NOT included: The library at the Weill Cornell Medical College in Qatar.
1, 2, 4	An estimate of the duplication between the Ithaca/Geneva and NYC campuses was excluded. Includes some open access items selected and cataloged in the OPAC to support research and educational needs.
2, 4	Increase reflects the addition of new titles, the addition of title-level records, better record categorization and the inclusion, for the first time, of almost 60,000 e-books created through CUL's collaboration with Google. Excludes more than 1.7 million e-books in the China Academic Digital Associative Library that are not cataloged at the title level in the OPAC. Includes some duplication between packages.
6	Includes $1,293,631 for grants tracked through the Office of Sponsored Programs.
7	The requested breakouts cannot be provided. Materials expenditures exclude Qatar's contribution to shared e-resources. FY14 materials expenditures include significant one-time expenditures.
8.a, 13.a	Includes academic and exempt staff.
8.b, 13.b	Includes non-academic, non-exempt staff.
9	General operating excludes $7,138,828 in building-related university allocated costs that became part of the library budget with the new Cornell budget model, which was designed to make campus expenditures more transparent.

QUESTION NUMBER	FOOTNOTE

CORNELL cont.

10   Does not include benefits paid directly by New York State for state employees. Includes $282,746 for grants tracked through the Office of Sponsored Programs. For the first time, the library's benefits reporting includes the library's share of Cornell Children's Tuition Scholarship expenditures, which were added to the library budget with the new Cornell budget model mentioned above.

11   The rate for staff on the endowed side of the Ithaca campus was 36%. The rate for the New York City campus was 31.7%.

13   Excludes any short-term temporary staff and any positions that were temporarily vacant on June 30, 2014. Includes 14.42 FTE for grant projects tracked through the Office of Sponsored Programs.

13.a   Includes academic and exempt staff.

13.b   Includes non-academic, non-exempt staff.

14, 15   Information transactions and presentations to groups include only those interactions staff recorded in Count It, CUL's locally built system for tracking public service transactions. Sessions related to the celebration of multiple special collections raised the presentations to groups counts, especially visible here in the number of participants.

16   Most service points collected full counts. Only three service points (circulation desks) sampled. Information transactions and presentations to groups include only those interactions staff recorded in Count It, CUL's locally built system for tracking public service transactions.

17   Includes ILL lending and Rare & Manuscript Collections transactions.

18   The count is for calendar year 2013. Includes counts for users in Qatar for subscriptions shared between campuses. Includes e-journal JR1 use (HTML and PDF) of resources of COUNTER-compliant publishers/vendors and some non-COUNTER-compliant vendors CUL tracked in previous years to retain consistency. The count attempts to remove any duplicate reporting between resources, and between campuses.

22   Traditional (vs. Borrow Direct) ILL includes some of the requests submitted by CUL patrons for items that were available at CUL.

24   This is the FY 2013 sum of the two NCES measures "Number of Doctor's degree-research/scholarship programs offered" and "Number of Doctor's degree-professional practice programs offered."

25   From this year on, this is NCES's measure "Instructional Staff". In 2011–2012 and 2012–2013, this figure additionally included the staff WCMC reported to NCES under "librarians, curators and archivists," as WCMC considers librarians instructional staff.

DARTMOUTH

    Library branches included: Baker-Berry Library, Feldberg Business & Engineering Library, Kresge Physical Sciences Library, Paddock Music Library, Rauner Special Collections, Sherman Art Library, and Storage Library.

4   Electronic books not counted as part of any individual library section, total overall for college is 731,574. Increasing digital collection.

7.c   A category of collection support that had not been included in the past is now being included.

9   Yearly fluctuations due to purchasing needs.

11   Fringe benefits at 34.5% include amounts for all regular and term employees. The fringe rate for temporary employees is 9%, and there is no fringe charged for student assistants.

12   NA

14, 15   Increased outreach and yearly fluctuations due to class needs.

QUESTION NUMBER	FOOTNOTE

DARTMOUTH cont.

16	Different methodologies of counting for FY 2014.
18–20	Figures are for the library system as a whole, not for any one branch so only recorded on the main report.
29	Raw numbers are more accurate than percentages due to the nature and size of the raw data. Part-time graduate students vary from year to year as non-degree participants are counted in this figure (employees, community members).

DELAWARE

10	For 2013–2014, the fringe benefit rate was 36.2% for professional staff (exempt employees), 63.9% for support staff (non-exempt employees), and 7.9% for graduate assistants. The University of Delaware offers an excellent benefits package, part of which includes comprehensive health care coverage and educational benefits, as well as a generous 403b retirement plan contribution for exempt employees and participation in the state pension plan for non-exempt staff. Detailed information about the benefits program can be found at http://www.udel.edu/Benefits/munu/index.html.
11	For 2013–2014, the fringe benefit rate for professional staff (exempt employees) was 36.2%.
17	Library online system does not provide a count of initial circulations, only total circulations. Reserve loans, however, have been excluded.
18	Information is not available.

DUKE

	Library branches included: Included in Main Library statistics: Perkins Library, Bostock Library, the Music Library, the Divinity School Library, Lilly Library, Pearse Memorial Library at the Duke University Marine Laboratory, David M. Rubenstein Rare-book & Manuscript Library. Included in Health Sciences Library statistics: Duke Medical Center Library. Included in Law Library statistics: Goodson Law Library. Included in the Special Collections statistics: David M. Rubenstein Rare-book & Manuscript Library.
	Library branches NOT included: Ford Library (Fuqua Business School).
7.c	FY 2014 actual figures higher than normal because of non-standard payment schedule.
8.b, 8.c	Support staff and student work salaries and wages are now combined, and will be in future years as well.
9	Reflects all expenses. Prior years netted out revenue and expenses; this new methodology considers total operating expenses less maintenance and fringes. In prior years Duke netted out collections expenditures here to avoid duplicate reporting from Collection Development.
11	26.3% is except staff; 25.6% non-exempt staff; 7.7% as applicable for students.
13.b	End-of-term appointments in two departments and the end of multiple one-off internships.
16	Reference transactions included all transactions in prior years. This year it is limited to those transactions classified as "research" transactions. The portion of transactions associated with chat reference was determined via sampling. We chose a sample week and categorized all chats as "research" or "other," then used the percentage that were research queries to calculate a number for all chats for reporting.
18–20	Duke Libraries is not providing responses to these three questions, as we do not have accurate data.
23–24	This number increased because the number of fields in which Doctor's degrees are awarded increased significantly.

EMORY

	All figures are as of 08/31/2014. [Main Library, Oxford College Library, and Theology Library]

QUESTION NUMBER	FOOTNOTE

EMORY cont.

Library branches included: Main, Health Sciences, Law, Oxford, Theology, and Special Collections.

Questions 1 and 18–20 are reported at the system level in the main library form. Question 4 is reported for Main, Oxford, and Theology combined. Health Sciences and Law are reported in the aggregated institutional totals in this publication, and they are also reported separately in the Law and Health Sciences publications. [Main Library]

11 — Editor's Note: Published figure reflects the official designated percent for the Law Library, as this is the maximum value entered for this question. [Main Library]

13 — Emory Libraries is now part of a combined library and IT organization. The positions reported in library professional and support staff represent those positions that are dedicated to support of library systems and operations without regard to reporting structure within the organization. [Main Library]

21 — Staffing issues affected acceptance of requests for fulfillment. [Main Library]

FLORIDA

Library branches included: Marston Science Library; Social Science and Humanities Library (Library West); Education Library; Architecture and Fine Arts Library.

4 — Increased number of e-books purchased for the collection in 2013–2014.

7.a — Decreased budget and purchase of print books because UF has moved collection focus to digital and patron driven acquisitions.

7.c — Decrease in spending due to decrease in binding materials.

11 — Represents fringe benefits percentage for librarians only.

13.c — Reduced budget for student assistants during 2013–2014.

14, 15 — UF reports presentations and participant numbers through an online system. We believe that this activity has been under reported for 2013–2014 and will continue instructing presenters to record their activities.

17 — Circulation activity for 2013–2014 shows continued trend of less use in print materials for UF patrons.

18 — Last year UF used an automated/canned report from 360 Counter that provided access counts of full-text requests for 39 aggregated platforms. This year, 2013–2014, UF performed a manual report from 16 publisher platforms (most heavily used) in order to provide a more accurate account of how UF patrons are accessing/using electronic resource collections.

19 — Last year UF reported the number of regular searches performed in individual databases based on COUNTER 3 Database Report 1 reports. UF thinks that the results provided using this technique inflated or duplicated search counts, particularly for databases on aggregator platforms. This year UF used COUNTER Platform Report 1 statistics that counted the number of regular searches performed across databases on various publisher and aggregator platforms. We think that the number provided for 2013–2014 better reflects the searching activities of patrons.

FLORIDA STATE

Library branches included: Main Library (Strozier); Dirac Science Library; College of Engineering Library; Allen Music Library; Goldstein College of Information Library; Ringling Museum of Art Library; Panama City, Panama Library; and Panama City, Florida Library.

The 2012–2013 survey mistakenly reported that the Florence and London branch libraries were included in the ARL Statistics. They are not members of ARL and should not have been included.

FLORIDA STATE cont.

2, 4	Last year the volume count for Main included electronic serials and documents as well as e-books and ETDs. This year only e-books and ETDs were counted; that is why there is a drop.
3	For the most part, the libraries used a bibliographic count to determine this number. However, the Florida State University Panama Branch Library used a physical count.
4	The significant drop in number is due to an issue with the number submitted in 2012–2013, which was 907,838. It should have been 79,904.
7.c	Ringling was the only library unable to submit a number this year, despite submitting one last year.
8	Various staff within the various branch libraries did experience salary changes, this was accounted for as best as was possible. While the total amount of money paid to staff decreased, the individual wages increased. The drop is due to a drop in library staffing.
8.a	What is considered support staff does vary between branch libraries. Also there were changes in staffing among the branch libraries, this was accounted for as best as was possible.
9	Several branch libraries did not have their figures for their other operating costs. Also, the libraries that were able to report their figures this year had lowered their operating expenditures.
10	Not all of the branch libraries included under the main library umbrella know the exact amount for the fringe benefits. For some libraries this is because it varies too much between individual employees. This number only includes the fringe benefits for Dirac, Strozier, Engineering, Panama City, and Music.
11	There are some slight differences among the different branch libraries. Several branch libraries do not know their exact number, and the Music Library actually designates 30%.
13.b	The branch libraries may have changed who they considered to be professional staff vs support staff. Also, there has been a trend over the last several years for the main library, in that each year has fewer staff than the year before.
14	Most of the branch libraries increased (Music and Ringling) the number of presentations they had.
14.a	For the most part, this number is not based on sampling, however the Florida State University Panama Branch library did use sampling to determine their numbers.
15	It may be that the presentations themselves are more tailored to smaller subjects/disciplines, which may result in fewer participants, or that the times of many of the presentations do not work for many students. The trend in this decrease appears across all library branches and there does not seem to be straightforward evidence of why this is happening.
15.a	For the most part, this figure is not based on representative sampling, however one of the branch libraries (Panama City, FL) did use representative sampling.
16	The drop is due to a new method of sampling in an effort to get a more accurate number. Under-reporting due to lack of staff may also contribute to the drop.
17	Several branch libraries began keeping better records of their initial circulations (i.e., Ringling). In previous years, there were issues where a significant portion of the circulations were not being counted.
18	This number does not include EBSCO searches. The EBSCO database searches for the number of full-text article requests (journals) could not be determined.
19	This number includes EBSCO database searches. The drop is because more people used One Search (a discovery tool) instead of going directly to the database.
20	This number includes EBSCO database searches. The increase could be due to the numbers being under-reported last year, because of a lack of access to reports.

Question Number	Footnote

FLORIDA STATE cont.

21	Seven loans were in process when the fiscal year ended. Those 7 are not included in the count.
22	Several factors contributed to the decrease in requests: change in the FSU Libraries' profile of resources available to the university community; liaisons outreach to graduates and faculty; and UBorrow continues to be more robust.
24	There are 75 doctoral degree programs, but over 160 majors within those programs. This number includes the professional programs offered. The previous year mistakenly counted the number of individual programs, the only year this had ever been done. This number is not including the ones for law and medical as to not double count the number of fields in which Doctor's degrees can be awarded.
25	The 2012–2013 year used incorrect data taken from the faculty headcount as opposed to the number from IPEDS, which is much more accurate. That is why there is such a drop in the number of instructional faculty. The 2012–2013 number for instructional faculty should have been 1,268, not 2,094.
26, 27	This number includes unclassified students.

GEORGE WASHINGTON

	Library branches included: The George Washington University Libraries, The Eckles Library at Mount Vernon Campus, The Virginia Science and Technology Library, and the Luther W. Brady Art Gallery.
1, 2, 4	Included consortially purchased EBSCO e-books and Springer titles, which were not included last year.
6	We underspent our materials budget in FY 2013 due to orders placed prior to the end of year, but the invoices did not arrive until the start of the new fiscal year. Additionally, GW Libraries was given a collections increase as a one-time increase for FY 2014.
13, 13.a	The new vice provost for libraries has been reshaping the GW Libraries staffing profile, which has led to vacant positions during FY 2014 that will now be filled in FY15 and FY16. Temporary staff have been hired in FY 2014 to cover gaps in professional staff positions.
16	Based on a stricter definition of "reference transaction" than used in previous years.
17	There has been a downward trend in circulation activity for the last few years primarily due to the steady increase in electronic resources and formats that are available.
22	Starting with FY 2014, we are not counting items received from the WRLC facility as part of this total, since many of these are GW-owned items.
23, 24	Including doctorates from our medical and law schools that were previously not counted.

GEORGETOWN

	Library branches included: Law, Medical, Bio-ethics Resource Center Library, Woodstock Theological Library, Blommer Science Library, SFS Qatar campus library.
2	FY 2014 large e-book purchase.
10	See http://benefits.georgetown.edu/
11	Editor's Note: Published figure reflects the official designated percent for the Health Sciences Library, as this is the maximum value entered for this question.
12	Correcting erroneous reporting in FY 2012–2013.
24	FY14 Corrects prior omissions.
27	Correcting undercount in FY 2013 figure.

GEORGIA

	All figures are as of 05/30/2014.

Question Number	Footnote

GEORGIA cont.

Library branches included: Main Library, Science Library, Special Collections Library.

GEORGIA TECH

Library branches included: Architecture Library.

GUELPH

All figures are as of 04/30/2014.

Library branches included: McLaughlin Library.

6–9, 10, 12	Expenditures as reported in Canadian dollars. Collections Expenditures: (7a) $1,598,590; (7b) $5,209,040; (7c) $858,631; (7) $7,666,261; Salary Expenditures: (8a) $4,816,680; (8b) $2,820,181; (8c) $186,119; (8) $7,822,980; (10) $2,208,708; Overall Expenditures: (7) $7,666,261; (8) $7,822,980; (9) $1,046,455; (6) $16,535,696; (12) NA/UA. NOTE: Total Salaries and Wages (Q8) EXCLUDES Fringe Benefits Expenditures (Q10).
7.b	Increased spending on electronic serials.
10	Movement of several position from "temporary" to "regular" staffed positions resulted in an increase in benefit expenditures. RFT positions have better benefits than TFT positions.
16	2013–2014 was the first full academic cycle under a new research help model.
18	The increase in number of article downloads, relative to last fiscal year, is likely due to a redesign of the library's website, with more searches being run on the Primo Central repository. Requests from 8,118 journals. The publishers (number of journals) are: Cambridge (332); Elsevier (2,129); Project Muse (603); Oxford (257); Sage (643); Wiley/Blackwell (1,867); and Springer/Kluwer (2,287).
19	On the library's website, the home page search box can be pointed to one or both of the library's catalogue and the Primo Central repository. The "journal articles" page search box points to the Primo Central repository. We cannot separate single database searches from federated ones.
20	Data available from Ex Libris (Primo) does not permit separation of library catalogue searches from Primo Central searches. Data is also not COUNTER compliant.
21, 22	Requests to and from other libraries have been declining year to year due to various programs and initiatives to enhance consortial buying and focus on e-resources.
23	RPA verifies these data as accurate. The number of PhDs conferred tend to be highly variable year to year.
24	Data not available.
29	2013–2014 RPA verifies this value as accurate.

HARVARD

Library branches included: Faculty of Arts and Sciences Libraries, Graduate School of Design Library (Loeb), Graduate School of Education Library (Gutman), Harvard Divinity School Library (Andover-Harvard Theological Library), Harvard Kennedy School Library, Radcliffe Library (Schlesinger), School of Engineering and Applied Sciences (SEAS), Harvard University Archives, and Villa I Tatti Library (Biblioteca Berenson).

Library branches NOT included: Harvard House Libraries, Property Information Center, and Harvard Development Office Library.

Efforts continue across campus to evaluate services to better develop efficiencies as a result of the reorganization of the libraries. This has directly impacted how some cost assessments are measured, as well as the scale of services such as internal document and resource delivery.

4	This is a university wide number and accounts for the aggregate total of e-books available to the campus. Due to cooperative purchasing of most of the e-book packages, it is impossible to break out numbers associated with branch campuses.

HARVARD cont.

6	During FY 2014, the libraries saw an overall increase in materials spending. This is the result of a combination of factors: endowment increases and expenditures, special one-time allocations of reserve funding, and improved processes to respond to orders and order processing.
7.c	Decreases in collection support can be directly attributed to shifts in how charges to libraries are assessed with respect to fees associated with the online catalog. Previously assessed specifically as a bibliographic utility charge, the charge is now assessed in aggregate with all fees assessed to libraries.
9	Due to changes in how bibliographic utilities are assessed to all libraries, the charge for this service is no longer separated out as a unique charge, which would have fallen under question 7c. Now, it is aggregated as part of a larger institution-wide library assessment for services held in common. As a result, this charge has been shifted and appears in this line, significantly increasing its total.
10	Fringe benefits include vacation salary, medical, dental, insurance, retirement, pensionable extra compensation, and non-pensionable extra compensation.
12	Charges assessed to support the online catalog are now rolled into a larger library assessment that does not differentiate this service.
13.c	This number is not available.
18–20	Data currently unavailable. Efforts are underway to examine measures to make this statistic available in the future.
24	There's been a recent revision of the mapping of programs to CIP codes, the taxonomy used by the Department of Education, which is mentioned in the ARL instructions, which has resulted in the increase in the number of codes we're using thus an increase in the total reported.
23–29	This is a university-wide number covering all schools and programs.

HAWAII

	The UH Manoa Library purchases some electronic resources for the John A. Burns School of Medicine Health Sciences Library and the William S. Richardson School of Law Library. These expenditures are included in the figures reported for UH Manoa Library.
4	Increase is due to increased emphasis on e-books.
7	Budget restrictions necessitated reduction of the materials budget.
7.a	Budget restrictions necessitated reduction of the monographs budget.
7.c	Budget restrictions necessitated reduced spending on collection support.
8.b	Budget restrictions necessitated leaving staff positions unfilled.
8.c	Budget restrictions necessitated reducing student worker hours.
12	Some memberships were canceled following a cost/benefit analysis.
13.a, 13.b	Centralized position control was implemented in FY2013. Vacant positions were eliminated from the library's position counts.
14	Reduced staff decreased capacity.
15	Class sizes increased.
16	There was a greater emphasis on data collection and gate counts have increased.
17	Continuing downward trend.
20	Adjustments were made to search interfaces and options.
21	Possibly due to participation in BorrowItNow.
23	Overall decline in student enrollment.

QUESTION NUMBER	FOOTNOTE

HOUSTON

All figures are as of 08/31/2014.

Library branches included: Architecture & Art Library, Music Library, Optometry Library.

4	The Libraries continue to increase their holdings in this area.
7.a	A larger percentage of the Libraries' collection budget is being used for ongoing resource purchases.
7.c	In FY 2013 the Libraries had significant purchases related to digitization efforts. Fewer funds were used in that area this year resulting in the overall decrease.

Collection Support Expenditures 2014:
ILL: $25,286
Security 3M: $17,018
TRAIL: $15,395
HathiTrust: $16,093
SIERRA–Innovative: $153,108
SUMMONS: $10,900
TMC: $342,408
CRL Membership: $54,935
YBP Marc Records: $6,980
Binding: $31,042
TexExpress: $4,076
Special Collections in-house bindery materials: $26,060
Exlibris for PRIMO: $71,499.36
Serials Solutions 360: $58,500
SFX Link Resolver: $24,664
Library Anywhere [Mobile catalog from ProQuest]: $2,080
ArcGIS: $2,000
EZ Proxy: $1,124
OCLC costs (total costs for resource sharing and cataloging): $215,681.49
ILL Scanners (one-time expense): $ 19,653
CONTENTdm–access to digital collections: $9,395
Docutek (e-reserves software): $10,911
OVID User License (access fee): $500
MYILIBRARY E-BOOKS (access fee): $500
EBSCO Service Charges to access packages: $26,789
MARCIVE (catalog records): $13,761
TDL: $0
LOCKSS: $0
Scanners for digitization: $0
TOTAL: $1,160,359

9	There is a reduction in the total expenditures resulting in a similar decrease in other operating expenditures.
10	The increase is directly related to the increased expenditures for salaries.
13.c	Last year we reported 57 FTE student assistants, but that number appears to be in error. The salary expenditures are comparable. Based on 2,080 work hours per year and using our standard salary for a student, the figure of 39 is more accurate.
14	This year, the Libraries instituted a technology training program for students. This resulted in the large increase in the number of classes.
18	The Libraries now use COUNTER 4 to gather these data and we believe this is responsible for the changes from last year.

Question Number	Footnote

HOWARD

Library branches included: The "Main Library" form provides information for the Architecture, Business, Divinity and Social Work Libraries and the special collection, Moorland Spingarn Research Center, which is also reported separately.

The electronic resources usage count includes data from the Health Sciences Library and the Law Library. The entire Howard community has access to the databases and online catalog maintained on a server at WRLC.

1 — The title count increased significantly because we imported 154,276 unique bibliographic records as a result of the OCLC Reclamation Project that was completed in Fiscal Year 2014.

4 — Library participated in a collaborative purchase program through the Washington Research Library Consortium that brought in a significant number of e-books.

7 — The library director's budget supported an energetic acquisitions program.

8.b — A reduction in force was mandated in January 2014.

9 — There was increased public programming and promotion thereof.

10 — The benefits include medical, dental and vision coverage, life insurance, disability benefits, and a retirement savings plan. Employees also have the option to enroll for commuter benefits, an Employee Assistance Program, long-term care benefits, a group legal program, and discount purchasing programs.

15 — More staff were involved in preparation and delivery of information literacy sessions.

15.a — The staff in the Public Affairs and Communications Office spearheaded effective advertisement and promotion of information literacy sessions.

16 — Staff collected data more consistently this year. More departments reported activity.

19 — Authentication issues were resolved, thereby enabling more users to access databases remotely. A new library website facilitated navigation for users with varying computer skills.

21, 22 — There were equipment and software problems during the year that hampered submission, transmission, and processing of ILL requests.

29 — Changes in policies.

ILLINOIS, CHICAGO

Library branches included: Richard J. Daley Library (main) and the following Health Sciences Libraries: Library of the Health Sciences-Chicago, Library of the Health Sciences-Peoria, Library of the Health Sciences-Rockford, and Library of the Health Sciences-Urbana.

2 — Daley Library has been focusing on weeding collections to create more space for users.

6 — The library's FY 2014 budget was increased by the provost. The university's budget office changed how it handles transfer of library/IT assessment funds; all funds are transferred to our budget at the beginning of the year rather than as spent. The FY 2014 transfer included unspent funds from previous years.

8 — Several faculty vacancies were filled in FY 2014. The university and the union representing faculty reached an agreement in FY 2014; retrospective salary payments for FY 2013 and FY 2014 are reflected in this expenditure.

9 — Amount includes $2.5 million transferred to plant funds.

10 — The library does not pay fringe benefits for staff paid from state accounts. Fringe benefit rate includes retirement (11.91%); health/life/dental insurance (23.85%). workers' comp. (0.01%); Medicare (1.45%); and terminal vacation/sick leave (1.13%) .

18–20 — Includes data for Richard J. Daley Library (main) and health sciences libraries.

28 — FY 2013 number included all graduate students, not just full-time.

ILLINOIS, URBANA

7.a	The increase in spending on one-time resources reflects purchase of major special collections, including the papers of poet Gwendolyn Brooks.
7.b	The decrease in spending for ongoing resources reflects an adjustment in our reporting. We no longer include recurring costs for non-collection items from this category.
8.a	Includes faculty, academic professionals, and pre-professional graduate assistants.
8.b	Includes permanent staff and temporary extra help employees.
8.c	Includes undergraduate students, grad hourly, and academic hourly employees. The decrease compared to FY 2013 reflects the reallocation of funds from temporary hourly positions to permanent civil service and academic professional positions.
11	Editor's Note: Published figure reflects the official designated percent for the Law Library, as this is the maximum value entered for this question.
12, 20	This information is not available.
13.a	Includes faculty, academic professionals, and graduate assistants.
13.b	Includes permanent civil service staff only.
13.c	Includes undergraduate students, grad hourly, and academic hourly employees.
16.a	The reference transactions total includes both continually logged data from some service points and extrapolations from sampled data from other service points.
17	Does not include Law Library. The 10.3% decrease continues a downward trend in the use of print collections.
18–20	Includes only data from EBSCO (723,586), Elsevier (2,064,862), and ProQuest (2,428,285). An increase in downloads of newspaper articles explains the increase overall compared to FY13.
19	Includes only data from EBSCO (33,416,085), Elsevier (1,169,528), and ProQuest (13,620,543). The COUNTER data shows a 21 million drop in EBSCO searches compared to last year, which we are investigating. At this time we cannot explain it.

INDIANA

	Library branches included: All IU Bloomington Libraries, IUB Law Library, and Special Collections (includes Lilly Library Rare-books Library and University Archives).
	Library branches NOT included: Ruth Lilly Medical Library.
4	Includes Congressional Serials Set: 381,121 volumes.
10	Covers retirement, health insurance, tuition benefit, life insurance, & workers compensation.
11	Official Designated Percent varies by employee type: 43.72% for professional staff, and 43.25% for support staff.
16	Due to remodeling projects in IUB's main library, several service desks were closed for significant portions of 2013–2014.
18–20	Because of incompatibilities within our reporting systems for electronic resources, we do not feel we can produce accurate use figures for this fiscal year. We are therefore not reporting data for lines 18–20.

IOWA

	Library branches included: Art, Business, Engineering, Music, and Sciences.
2	Probable batch load/batch change issues creating significant increase; we cannot determine at this time.
8.a, 13.a	Includes a coordinator and IT programming staff that support the Libraries but not paid directly from Libraries' budget.

Question Number	Footnote
IOWA cont.	
11	Rate for professional & scientific classification .
IOWA STATE	
	Library branches included: Iowa State University Library–Parks Library (Main Library), Veterinary Medical Library, and Special Collections data is also included in this survey.
1	Titles held increased due to the purchase of large e-book backfile collections.
2	One-time adjustment is due to a more accurate count method due to staffing change.
7.a	Funds were reallocated in this fiscal year to put towards one-time electronic resource purchases.
7.c	In FY 2013, document delivery expenditures were not included in the collections support total and in FY 2014 it was included.
11	Faculty 31.5%; Professional & Scientific 37.8%; and Merit 50%.
13.a	Decrease in professional staff due to retirements and resignations.
13.b	Increase in support staff, FTE due to new hires in the library into support positions.
18	Last year we gave a number that was a reflection of total requests, in FY 2014 it reflected the number of successful requests.
22	One-time adjustment is due to a more accurate counting method due to staffing change.
JOHNS HOPKINS	
	Library branches included: Milton S. Eisenhower, Welch, History of Medicine, Friedheim, and SAIS.
6	Reflects an increase in operating costs from our decentralized environment.
KANSAS	
	Library branches included: Main campus libraries (Lawrence, KS) and Regents Center Library (Overland Park, KS).
7.a	FY 2014 totals include significantly higher expenditures on major purchases than FY 2013.
7.c	In FY 2014, the collections budget took on responsibility for OCLC costs.
8.a, 8.b	Change due to campus-wide reclassification of many support staff to professional staff.
10	Includes SS, retirements, leave, insurance, local tax, and parking.
11	Annual fringe percentage is 18.758% plus $6,275 annually for health insurance.
13.a, 13.b	Beginning in 2013–2014, we changed the methodology that we use to report professional staff. Unclassified professional staff are now reported in the support staff category, rather than the professional staff category. [Lawrence Campus]
16	KU Info stats are not included as in previous years. FY 2013 number for KU Info was 64,500.
18–20	Possible reasons for decline in searches: (1) Usage system errors and/or calculation issues in prior or current year; (2) complications resulting from format change from COUNTER (R3) to COUNTER (R4); (3) Discovery system reliance on link resolver and link resolver failures; (4) platform and/or interface changes (i.e., CSA Illimina, EBSCO interface October 2013; ProQuest (LAD) platform change to ProQuest (PAM), which was excluded due to overcount; (5) cancellations; (6) actual usage declines.
23	Over the past six years we've had some graduate class increases and the larger classes are now finishing their degrees.
KENT STATE	
	Library branches included: Performing Arts, Architecture, Map, and Fashion.
1, 2	Decrease due to weeding activities.

QUESTION NUMBER	FOOTNOTE

KENT STATE cont.

10	Medical, dental, prescription, vision, long-term and short-term disability, and life insurance coverage, leave time, tuition remission, and retirement.
12	Calculated this by multiplying current FTE from RPIE by a per/FTE amount from OhioLINK; last year's data was extrapolated.
17	This year's figure includes in-house-use-counts for the first time in addition to regular check-outs.

KENTUCKY

	Library branches included: Agricultural Information Center, Design Library, Education Library, Little Fine Arts Library, Law Library, Medical Center Library, Morris Equine Library, Science Library, Shaver Engineering Library, Special Collections Library, Transportation Library, and William T. Young Library (main library).
1, 2	Total titles held and volumes held for the main library includes medical library.
4	Total electronic books increased substantially due to enhanced access/discoverability for e-books. Main library total for electronic books also includes the medical library e-books.
7.a	Increase due to purchase of additional JSTOR Collections (Arts & Sciences IX, X, XI, Business IV) using endowment funds.
10	Includes retirement, health insurance, life insurance, and miscellaneous fringe benefits (FICA and Social Security)
18–19	Total for the main library also includes the medical library.

LAVAL

	All figures are as of 04/30/2014.
	Library branches included: All branches included.
1, 4	We have removed the ProQuest thesis collection that was included in the past, and we rewrote the report procedure in Sirsi-Workflow to reflect new type of catalogue titles.
2	In 2012–2013 the total number of volumes held should have been 5,315,812, not 6,7752,30. The reason for this year's decrease is that we have removed from the catalogue all the slides, maps, and other items no longer available.
6–9, 10, 12	Expenditures as reported in Canadian dollars. Collections Expenditures: (7a) $2,941,618; (7b) $9,429,237; (7c) $425,755; (7) $12,796,610; Salary Expenditures: (8a) $4,639,390; (8b) $6,314,441; (8c) $0; (8) $10,953,831; (10) $2,874,847; Overall Expenditures: (7) $12,796,610; (8) $10,953,831; (9) $790,732; (6) $24,541,173; (12) NA/UA. NOTE: Total Salaries and Wages (Q8) EXCLUDES Fringe Benefits Expenditures (Q10).
7	We did transfer a significant amount of budget from one-time purchase to subscriptions due to increase subscription fees and decreasing value of Canadian dollar.
8, 13	We no longer hire students.
9	We had a decrease to this budget.
24	We have 74 programs in 16 faculties in which PhD can be awarded.
10	Includes pension and health care.
11	Support staff 36.32%, professional and directors 19.70%, and temporary staff 12.71%.
26–29	The number here is Full Time Equivalent.

QUESTION NUMBER	FOOTNOTE

LOUISIANA STATE

	Library branches included: The "Main Library" report includes statistics for Special Collections, which is a branch library. Statistics for the Veterinary Medicine Library and the LSU Law Library, which are on the same campus with the LSU Libraries ("Main Library") but are administered separately, are included in the aggregated institutional totals in this publication, and they are also reported separately in the Law and Health Sciences publications.
1	This count does not include the estimated 2.9 million pre-1976 government document titles lacking bibliographic records.
2	This count does not include the estimated 2.9 million pre-1976 government document titles lacking bibliographic records. Volume counts for these titles will be added as the collection is retrospectively cataloged. This volume count does include 1,820 "volumes" calculated based on the number of linear feet of added archival and manuscript material. LSU Libraries added 182 linear feet of archival collections, so at 10 "traditional" volumes per foot, that is the equivalent of 1,820 volumes. This volume count includes 10,068 "volumes" added calculated based on a corrected use of the formulae "5.2 documents pieces per volume (per ARL)" for our government documents department. Previous reports of government documents volumes were done erroneously and the process has now been corrected.
3	The basis of count is a combination of physical and bibliographic.
8.a	This number includes librarians in faculty positions and salaried personnel >$50k/annum.
8.b	This number includes civil service, library assistants, professional/unclassified, and 7 FTE graduate assistants.
10	Fringe benefits in dollars for the main library report calculated as follows: Step 1: Professional and support staff wages calculated as 8a plus 8b minus 138,954 graduate student wages, a total of 4,262,951. Step 2: Calculate fringe percentage based on July 01, 2014 fringe benefit rates–40% of 4,262,951; which equals 1,705,180; and 3% of 138,954; which equals 4,169. Step 3: Calculate total fringe percentage by summing 1,705,180 plus 4,169; which equals 1,709,349 for the main library.
11	Effective July 01, 2014, fringe benefit rates for regular salaried positions is 40% and for graduate assistants it's 3%.
12	This is the LSU portion of the monies given by the BoR to the LOUIS Consortium. In fiscal year 2014, Regents gave LOUIS $500,000. LSU used the following formula to calculate our portion of the 500,000 amount for the main library: (LSU FTE / Total FTE of public academics)* total amount given to LOUIS Consortium. LSU's FTE = 34,393. (34,393/205,681)*500,000 = $83,607 for the main library.
13.a	This number includes librarians in faculty positions and salaried personnel >$50k/annum.
13.b	This number includes civil service, library assistants, professional/unclassified, and 7 FTE graduate assistants.
16	Research desk statistics were taken three times in fiscal year 2013–2014, and this number is an average of those three weeks multiplied by 34 to exclude the slow summer months, holiday periods, and intersession periods and to keep statistics consistent with previous years.
18	This number is derived from COUNTER data.
19	Last year (2012–2013) this number reflected the discovery layer and was reported by the vendor in COUNTER form as "regular" searches. This year that same vendor has reported this year's data as "federated searches." This number was derived from several COUNTER reports.
20	This number reflects resources within a discovery service. Last year (2012–2013) a majority of this data was reported in Q 19 as that is where the vendor supplied the data in the COUNTER report.

Question Number	Footnote

LOUISVILLE

	Library branches included: Main, Archives & Special Collections, Art, Law (collections, circulation, and staff data only), and Music. Health Sciences data is included in the aggregated institutional totals in this publication, and those data are also reported separately in the Health Sciences publication.
10	Fringe benefits include health insurance; retirement plan; vacation, sick and holiday leave; education benefits for employees and dependents; retiree benefits; and wellness program.
12	Same figure as last year.
13	An incentive retirement program had an impact on our professional staffing.
15	Figure for 2012–2013 is incorrect, which makes the increase over the past year appear to be much higher than it actually is. The 12,611 figure is the total from 2010–2011. The figure for last year should have been 19,788.
19	Decline from last year can be attributed to implementation of WorldCat Local at the end of calendar year 2013. Use of this approach reduces the need for regular database searches.
20	Significant difference from last year's figure is due to implementation of WorldCat Local at the end of the 2013 calendar year. Federated searches prior to this time were accomplished through Voyager MetaLib which was not a high-use approach. All WCL searches are federated searches and are easily measured.

MCGILL

	All figures are as of 04/30/2014.
	Library branches included: Birks Reading Room (religious studies), Education Curriculum Resources Centre, Islamic Studies, Life Sciences, Osler (history and social sciences of medicine), Humanities and Social Sciences (includes management and education), Blackader-Lauterman (art, architecture), Marvin Duchow Music, Nahum Gelber Law, Rare-books and Special Collections, McGill University Archives, Schulich Library of Science and Engineering, Macdonald Campus, Edward Rosenthall Mathematics and Statistics.
4	This number represents e-book titles that are in our catalogue for the 2013–2014.
6–9, 10, 12	Expenditures as reported in Canadian dollars. Collections Expenditures: (7a) $4,391,730; (7b) $13,441,491; (7c) $0; (7) $17,833,221; Salary Expenditures: (8a) $5,512,002; (8b) $7,021,990; (8c) $262,935; (8) $12,796,927; (10) $2,083,053; Overall Expenditures: (7) $17,833,221; (8) $12,796,927; (9) $3,964,964; (6) $34,595,112; (12) NA/UA. NOTE: Total Salaries and Wages (Q8) EXCLUDES Fringe Benefits Expenditures (Q10).
10	Includes vacation, health and dental benefits, and pension.
12	Consortial and network expenditures are included in 7b.
13.b	Reduction due to voluntary retirement program in August 2013.
15, 16	New measure.
16.a	A portion of reference statistics was obtained using sampling.
21	Slight reduction due to portion of collection being unavailable during relocation.
22	Slight increase to due portion of collection being unavailable during relocation.
23	Includes PhDs, doctorates, medical, dentistry, and law degrees.

MCMASTER

	All figures are as of 04/30/2014.
	Library branches included: Mills Memorial Library, H.G. Thode Library of Science & Engineering, and Innis (Business) Library.

Question Number	Footnote

MCMASTER cont.

6–9, 10, 12 Expenditures as reported in Canadian dollars. Collections Expenditures: (7a) $804,546; (7b) $7,914,191; (7c) $1,036,348; (7) $9,755,085; Salary Expenditures: (8a) $3,721,093; (8b) $3,026,354; (8c) $244,211; (8) $6,991,658; (10) $2,748,307; Overall Expenditures: (7) $9,755,085; (8) $6,991,658; (9) $970,600; (6) $17,717,343; (12) $2,210. NOTE: Total Salaries and Wages (Q8) EXCLUDES Fringe Benefits Expenditures (Q10).

10 Includes Statutory CPP, EI, EHT, WSIB; pension; dental; major medical; life insurance; surcharge; post-retirement surcharge; WSIB NEER surcharge; and sick leave pool for permanent staff.

11 Percentages are based on pay group, e.g., Unifor, TMG, faculty, etc., as well as salary range. Average is 42%.

MANITOBA

All figures are as of 03/31/2014.

Library branches included: All branches.

6–9, 10, 12 Expenditures as reported in Canadian dollars. Collections Expenditures: (7a) $2,383,540; (7b) $6,995,172; (7c) $690,878; (7) $10,069,590; Salary Expenditures: (8a) $5,970,004; (8b) $5,243,492; (8c) $884,136; (8) $12,097,632; (10) $2,403,340; Overall Expenditures: (7) $10,069,590; (8) $12,097,632; (9) $2,787,458; (6) $24,954,680; (12) NA/UA. NOTE: Total Salaries and Wages (Q8) EXCLUDES Fringe Benefits Expenditures (Q10).

MARYLAND

Library branches included: McKeldin Library (main library), Architecture Library, Art Library, Engineering & Physical Sciences Library, Hornbake Library, Michelle Smith Performing Arts Library, Priddy Library (Universities at Shady Grove), and White Memorial Chemistry Library.

2 Volumes remain undercounted: we are unable to estimate volumes in special collections and government documents. Focus on acquiring e-resources.

16 FY 2012 and FY 2013 were transition years to a new non-sampling system. FY 2014 data should be more accurate, though may still be underreported.

17 Short-term loans like equipment were excluded. Equipment loans were 87,074.

21 Increase due to increased ILL staffing and implementation of more efficient procedures.

22 Increase likely due to the use of ILL to supplement currently unavailable sections in the Libraries (e.g., 5th floor stacks and architecture folios) and the promotion of UBorrow as an alternative to recalls.

MASSACHUSETTS

Library branches included: Image Library, and Sciences & Engineering Library.

4 631,207 print items were removed from the Government Documents collection and were replaced by electronic access to GPO.

7.a The changing nature of our purchasing program allowed for catching up on some one-time material that should have been acquired in recent years.

8.c Last year's report of student assistants FTE was in error. This year's student FTE represents a 10% increase over FY 2013. The expenditures reported for student assistants in FY 2013 were accurate.

MASSACHUSETTS cont.

10, 11   Reported fringe benefit costs are for a small number of staff whose salaries/wages are not funded from state appropriations. The fringe costs for state-funded staff is unknown and is funded by a legislative appropriation directly to the state retirement board and insurance board. The amount of that general appropriation that is attributable to the university is unknown, so the amount for library staff cannot be calculated. University departments with staff from other than state appropriations are charged varying rates for fringe benefits depending on the funding source. That range of rates averages approximately 28.3%, but that average cannot be imputed as the rate for all state-funded positions due to lack of sufficient information on which to make an estimate.

14, 15   Includes sessions and participants taught by TAs in English 112 who were trained by the reference staff. The increase in sessions also reflects two staff members who returned from sabbatical leave during the previous year.

17   Increasingly, students are using digital content and relying less on print materials.

19   More vendors in our broader group of suppliers of digital information are conforming to COUNTER guidelines, and users are increasingly leaning toward networked content.

22   Increased digital content has reduced the number of items we need to acquire from external sources.

MIT

Library branches included: All libraries at MIT are included in the ARL Statistics. This includes all special collections as well.

7.c   Categories include contract binding, document delivery/ILL, outsourced cataloging.

13   One department, Academic Media Production Services (AMPS), was moved into a non-Libraries department as of 7/1/13, causing a drop in staff numbers.

19   Searches via EBSCO Discovery Service, launched in FY 2014, included in COUNTER Reports.

20   Metalib, our federated search tool, was discontinued in FY 2014.

21   This figure includes interlibrary loans, as well as loans through the Boston Library Consortium and BorrowDirect partnerships.

MIAMI

All figures are as of 05/31/2014. [Central Library (Richter) and Marine Library]

Library branches included: Business, Architecture, and Music Library data are included in the Richter (Central) Library statistics. Marine, Law, and Calder Medical Library data are included in the aggregated institutional totals in this publication for the University of Miami Libraries. [Central Library (Richter)]

9   No significant renovation or collection movement projects in FY2014. [Central Library (Richter)]

11   Professional staff fringe rates vary. [Central Library (Richter)]

19   Revised method and new resources used to obtain more accurate database search data. [Central Library (Richter)]

MICHIGAN

Library branches included: University Library, Bentley Historical Library, William L. Clements Library, Kresge Business Administration Library, and the Law Library.

Library branches NOT included: Dearborn and Flint campuses.

Data from the Health Sciences Library is included in the figures reported.

MICHIGAN STATE

Library branches included: Gull Lake, Business, Engineering, and Mathematics.

MICHIGAN STATE cont.

1	Started with number of bib records in database as of 7/1/14 (8,023,231), subtracted HathiTrust and CRL records (1,488,336) and then subtracted volumes withdrawn during the 2012–2013 fiscal year (3,750). Total = 6,531,145. This number is significantly less than last year's reported number because we are not including HathiTrust and CRL e-book numbers, as we did last year.
2	Includes the following: Total print vol. count for 2012–2013 = 4,966,566. To this we added print cataloging for 2013–2014 (26,375) and all e-books except HathiTrust and CRL (1,555,710). Total volumes held for June 30 = 6,548,621.
4	E-book count as of June 30, 2014, (less HathiTrust and CRL e-books) is 1,555,710. Total of packages as follows: Serials Solutions 317,953; Serial Set 320,012; ERIC 226,201; English Short Title Catalog 137,964; Early English Books Online 119,619; Lexis Nexis Congressional Hearings 106,004; Sabin 42,144; Office of Scientific & Tech. Info. 41,680; Nineteen Century Collections Online 29,742; Literature Online 14,727; Alexander Street Press 10,132; Electronic theses 7,737; All other e-book packages 183,159.
7.c	Includes: Binding ($141,397.36); ILL ($52,211.96); Postage ($ 5,162.37); Preservation ($17,935.73); FEE ($33,005.34); Memberships ($201,383.90); Services ($171,291.00).
10, 11	Fringes are paid by the university, not the library. This cost cannot be estimated because the fringe benefits percentage rate varies depending on salary.
11	Editor's Note: Published figure reflects the official designated percent for the Law Library, as this is the maximum value entered for this question.
18	This number is somewhat lower than last year as some reports have moved to COUNTER 4 and data prior to 2014 could not be obtained.
19	This number is substantially higher than last year because of a large increase in searches for one of our major vendor platforms. Accuracy of the data was confirmed for both time periods with the vendor, but there was no apparent explanation for the large increase.
23	Simply more degrees earned and awarded than the previous year.

MINNESOTA

	Library branches included: List at https://www.lib.umn.edu/about/collections.
2, 4	We migrated from the Aleph ILS to Alma, which necessitated record cleanup that clarified our holdings.
4	More e-book packages were purchased last FY.
8.a, 13.a	Special projects funding.
15	Expanded instructional offerings.
16	Consolidation of service desks in all of our main libraries.
20	Migration from Metalib to Primo Central as our discovery service.
24	Methods for obtaining the number of fields available for Doctorate-level awards were improved to capture some that may have been missing in prior years.

MISSOURI

	Library branches included: Main Library, Math Library, Engineering Library, Geology Library, Journalism Library, Veterinary Medical Library, Health Sciences Library, University Archives, and Libraries Depository.
2	Increase in library holdings.
9	Includes library system expended funds now part of budget allocation. Additional expenses due to mold damage at one of the remote storage facilities.
14	Decrease in number of presentations from previous year, increase in participants.

QUESTION NUMBER	FOOTNOTE

MISSOURI cont.

18   Data from publishers and aggregated databases.

19   Data from publishers and vendors for databases and e-journals. Data was adjusted to remove estimated widget usage.

20   MU Libraries does not subscribe to a federated search service. However, we do subscribe to a discovery tool (Summon). For FY 2014 there were 762,311 searches of Summon.

23   Enrollment increase.

MONTREAL

All figures are as of 04/30/2013 [Bibliothèques UdeM, École Polytechnique de Montréal, and HEC Montréal].

Aménagement, Botanique, Campus de Laval, Cartothèque, Chimie, Didacthèque, ÉPC-Biologie, Géographie, Kinésiologie, Lettres et sciences humaines, Livres rares et collections spéciales, Mathématiques et informatique, Médecine vétérinaire, Musique, Optométrie, Physique, École Polytechnique Library, HEC Montréal Library, Law (Droit), and Health Science Libraries (Santé).

6–9, 10, 12   Expenditures as reported in Canadian dollars. Collections Expenditures: (7a) $2,206,630; (7b) $10,864,181; (7c) $323,044; (7) $13,393,855; Salary Expenditures: (8a) $9,143,420; (8b) $10,363,511; (8c) $155,535; (8) $19,662,466; (10) $5,286,858; Overall Expenditures: (7) $13,393,855; (8) $19,662,466; (9) $2,127,369; (6) $35,183,690; (12) $44,491. NOTE: Total Salaries and Wages (Q8) EXCLUDES Fringe Benefits Expenditures (Q10).

13.b   Total support staff for last year (2012–2013 survey) revised to 153. [Bibliothéques UdeM]

NEBRASKA

Library branches included: Architecture, C.Y. Thompson, Engineering, Geology, Law, Math, and Music.

10   Fringe Benefits include FICA, health insurance, life insurance, and retirement.

18, 19   UNL has acquired many new database packages and statistics are being collected differently effective January 2014.

NEW MEXICO

Library branches included: Centennial Science & Engineering Library, Fine Arts & Design Library, Parish Memorial Library, and Zimmerman Library.

4   University Libraries changed policy to default in many cases to e-books.

7.b   Purchased additional databases.

8, 8.a   Redefined professional vs. support roles.

11   29% for faculty; 32.5% for staff. Editor's Note: Published figure reflects the official designated percent for the Law Library, as this is the maximum value entered for this question.

13–13.b   Redefined professional vs. support roles.

NEW YORK

6   Variance due to growth of new campuses in Shanghai and Poly.

7.a   Variance due to merger of Poly School of Engineering.

7.c   Variance due to additional bibliographic management tools acquired.

8   Salary expenditures are understated in 2013–2014 because salary data for Shanghai-based staff was not available.

8.a, 8.b   Variance due to the inclusion of Shanghai (NY-based staff only, Shanghai-based staff data not available) and Poly School of Engineering, and also the growth at Abu Dhabi.

Question Number	Footnote

NEW YORK cont.

10	Variance due to the inclusion of Shanghai (NY-based staff only) and Poly School of Engineering, and also the growth at Abu Dhabi.
11	Editor's Note: Published figure reflects the official designated percent for the Health Sciences Library, as this is the maximum value entered for this question.
13.a, 13.b	Variance due to the addition of Poly School of Engineering staff in NY, and growth at Abu Dhabi and Shanghai portal campuses.
15	Blended services and instruction provided by the Digital Studio previously not reported in FY 2013 is now included in FY 2014.
19	More COUNTER-compliant vendor data available in FY 2014.
22	Total user requests decline due to decrease in fill rate from 82.4% in FY 2013 to 79.5% in FY 2014.
24	General university trend.
25	Variance due to the inclusion of Shanghai and Abu Dhabi instructional faculty data.

NORTH CAROLINA

	Library branches included: Davis Main, Undergraduate Library, Wilson Special Collections Library, Music Library, Kenan Science Library, Art Library, School of Information and Library Science Library, School of Government Library, Marine Science Library, Stone Center Library, Carolina Digital Library and Archives, Law Library, and Health Sciences Library.
1	Total listed includes only titles in book format.
7.a-7.c	Decrease due to receipt of one-time year-end funding for additional materials purchases in previous year.
11	The university designates 22.04% + fixed health insurance of $5,192.
18, 19	Total listed represents usage from January to December 2012.
21	Statistics exclude requests filled from UNC collections for distance education students, as well as requests filled from UNC databases, e-journals, e-books, and from the Internet.

NORTH CAROLINA STATE

	Library branches included: Main campus libraries: D.H. Hill and James B. Hunt Jr.; Library Branches: Design, Natural Resources, Veterinary Medicine, African-American Cultural Center, and College of Education Media and Educational Technology and Research Center.
6, 9	In its first year of operation, in FY 2013, the James B. Hunt Jr. Library cost an additional $4,000,000 in one-time funds.
7.a	Decrease due to receipt of one-time provost's allocation of $700,500 in FY 2013.
7.c	Includes bibliographic utilities, document delivery, association memberships, storage, and binding expenditures.
10, 11	Faculty/staff fringe benefits rate is 30%. Graduate assistant fringe benefits rate is 15%. Undergraduates fringe benefits rate is 0.80%
13.b	Decrease in staff FTE due to budget reductions.
14	Increase in instruction sessions due to additional graduate student and research workshops, plus demand for undergraduate instruction following tours and orientation activities.
15	Increase in number of participants corresponds to increase in sessions.
16	Decrease in activity at the College of Education Media and Education Technology and Research Center.
16.a	Are in the process of moving to 100% actual count for all libraries. Current methodology is a mixture of sampling (two branches) and actual (two main libraries and three branches).

NORTH CAROLINA STATE cont.

20   Increase in federated searches due to increased use of the Summon discovery service.

22   Due to increase in demand for articles not supported through local subscriptions.

25   FY 2012–2013 figure revised to 1,775.

NORTHWESTERN

All figures are as of 08/31/2014.

Library branches NOT included: Northwestern Qatar is not included in collections count this year since the purchasing model for collections is for Northwestern Qatar only. Northwestern Qatar expenditures and other figures were not included in previous years.

1, 2   This total does not include NU-Qatar this year. The purchasing model for NU-Qatar collections is only for NU-Qatar and very few titles besides some e-books are currently available to Northwestern University.

4   The loading of MARC record sets for packages of content remained more consistent while also increasing in volume.

7.c   There were fewer items provided through document delivery, perhaps because of popularity of consortial borrowing expansion among wider group of supplier libraries.

10   Fringe benefit amount is actual amount charged for reported salary expense.

13.a   Vacant positions were filled, but no new staff lines were added.

14, 15   Africana Library did not keep count this past year so figures are from previous year. Outreach activities by other units were expanded and increased, and were very successful in increasing participation in addition to having more presentations.

16   Repositioning of the main reference desk to make room for repurposing of space increased visibility and traffic counts. Outreach activities from other units were very successful in increasing use of services.

17   Circulation statistics trend downwards as more resources become available online.

18, 19, 20   Lower use of online resources from previous peak years could have multiple yet hard to confirm reasons, such as multiple paths to resources that may not always be accurately counted, better discovery instead of blind searching, and better focus on use of applicable resources.

20   Discovery layers trump federated search software in today's search environment.

22   A new consortial borrowing service expanded the supplier library list with reliable and fast delivery service.

23, 24   Not reported for 2012–2013.

25   The count this year was counted by major school from the latest data available.

NOTRE DAME

Library branches included: The Theodore M. Hesburgh Library (Main Library) (library.nd.edu) also includes the Center for Digital Scholarship, Medieval Institute Library (library.nd.edu/medieval), and Rare-books and Special Collections (rare-books.library.nd.edu). BRANCH LIBRARIES of the Hesburgh Libraries include eight other libraries on campus: Architecture Library (library.nd.edu/architecture), Mahaffey Business Library (library.nd.edu/business), Chemistry-Physics Library (library.nd.edu/chemistry, library.nd.edu/physics), Engineering Library (library.nd.edu/engineering), Kellogg Kroc Library (library.nd.edu/Kellogg Kroc), O'Meara Mathematics Library (library.nd.edu/mathematics), Radiation Chemistry Reading Room (library.nd.edu/radiology lab) and Visual Resources Center (library.nd.edu/visual resource center).Also included in the statistics for the University of Notre Dame Libraries are the Notre Dame Law School's Kresge Law Library (law.nd.edu/library) and University Archives. [Main Library].

NOTRE DAME cont.

	Library branches included: Archives of the University of Notre Dame [University Archives].
	Library branches NOT included: International locations such as Notre Dame's Rome Library have not been included. [Main Library]
1	The "Titles held" figure of 1,503 represents the number of manuscript collections and university records series held by the Archives. These collections and series vary in size from one sheet of paper to several thousand boxes and consist, variously, of manuscripts, printed materials (including in some cases thousands of books), ephemera, microfilm, AV items, photographs, digital files, and artifacts. Altogether, our collections contain almost 41,000 linear feet of materials. [University Archives]
2	The number of "Volumes held" as defined in the instructions is impossible to accurately estimate without spending an unwarranted amount of time. [University Archives]
4	Approximately 140,800 additional e-books were added to the catalog during the fiscal year due to increasing availability of resources in this format. [Main Library]
7.c	Collection support expenditures consist primarily of memberships for the purpose of obtaining/accessing publications and literature searching plus Interlibrary Loan and Binding. An increase in collection support expenditures of approximately $75,000 is due to an additional payments for ILL shared resources. [Main Library]
8.a, 8.b	Professional staff expenditures have increased and support staff decreased due to the inclusion of non-faculty professional staff in the expenditures for this line rather than the support staff line. Both the FTE and expenditures related to certain professional staff were reported in the support staff lines in the prior year. Had the expenditures for these 17 FTE's been included in the professional staff line in the 2012–2013 fiscal year, the difference would have been an increase of only 2.2% for professional staff and a decrease of 8.6% for support staff. [Main Library]
9	For the Main libraries, the increase in other library operating expenditures was a result of increases in several categories. The most notable were expenditures for a newly created center for digital scholarship that provides training and assistance to students and researchers using technology. [Main Library]
9	Other operating expenditures includes supplies for housing collections (mainly boxes, folders, and sleeves), shipping for donated collections, capital equipment, repair and maintenance, postage, duplication, office supplies, and all other non-salary expenditures. [University Archives]
10	Fringe benefits include employer's share of government taxes (FICA, SS, SSI, FUTA (unemployment), worker's comp, etc.), as well as health insurance and retirement benefits for eligible employees. [Main Library and University Archives]
11	Fringe benefit rates vary by employee class, therefore the rate for full-time librarians (faculty) 26.7% has been reported. The rate for full-time exempt staff and professionals is 31% and full-time non-exempt staff is 48.9%. Rates for part-time employees vary from 2% for student employees to 16.9% for part-time staff and faculty (librarians). [Main Library]
11	We believe the official designated percentages are still 27.1% for professional staff, 41.7% for support staff, 7.9% for on-call staff, and 1.3% for student workers. [University Archives]
12	Access to resources has not been paid from centrally-funded systems or from arrangements where the library does not pay fully/and or directly. This amount was incorrectly reported in the prior year(s). [Main Library]

NOTRE DAME cont.

13.a, 13.b	Professional staff FTE has increased by 15% primarily due to an increase in non-faculty professional staff in high-level technical and digital resource positions. These staff and others whose positions require post-baccalaureate degrees were reclassified from support staff to professional staff, a total of 17 FTE. [Main Library]
14, 15	The number of instruction classes and participants has decreased due to less accurate and inconsistent reporting of instruction activities. [Main Library]
16	Reference transactions have been clarified and tracked consistently. [Main Library]
16.a	The "Number of reference transactions" figure is based half on counts and half on extrapolation. [University Archives]
21	The interlibrary loan reporting structure was reorganized resulting in additional employees to fill requests. [Main Library]
22	Lending requests filled dropped by 25% due in part to the decrease in requests for materials received and a large drop in OCLC articles filled. The decreased fill rates were due in part to the unavailability of material requested that was frequently charged out to our own users. [Main Library]
23	The 2013–2014 count is based upon the Registrar's curricula listing that more narrowly defines the field for Doctor's degrees. For example, History was defined as a field in the prior year and according to the Registrar, there are actually four fields in the history department. [Main Library]
25	Increase in faculty is due to expansion of degree programs. [Main Library]
27	Due to the small number of part-time students that enroll each year, the entire change in this statistic results from a variation of 30 students resulting in an increase of 16%. Full-time enrollment decreased in both the undergrad and graduate level. The overall increase in the FTE student enrollment was two students and 0%. [Main Library]

OHIO

	Library branches included: OU-HCOM-LRC (Athens and Dublin campuses) and regional campuses (Chillicothe, Zanesville, Eastern, Southern, Lancaster).
7.a	Typical end-of-year high dollar backfile purchases delayed to FY15. FY14 purchased Oxford University Press Journal Archives ($217K). FY14 one-time cost for JSTOR scholarly journal archive ($75K).
7.b	Clinical key renewal expense ($59K) deferred to FY15 by university controller.
7.c	Journal binding costs declined $9K. Regional campus technical service costs declined $10K. Athens campus technical service costs declined.
8.b	Decline partially due to FY 2013 figure inflated due to change in central accounting procedures for accrued hourly payroll resulting in a 27th 2-week pay.
10	Health insurance $836,551 ($12,029/employee excluding P-T students); Retirement $575,652 (14%, student employees are exempted when actively enrolled in coursework); Worker's compensation $33,199 (0.739% for all employees); Medicare $52,355 (1.45% for employees hired after March 31, 1986. IN FY 2013–2014, one professional and five support staff were exempt); Employee uniforms $158; and Accrued benefits (includes all categories except health insurance) $938.
11	Percentage for full-time staff only: Retirement (14%)—student employees are exempted when actively enrolled in coursework; Worker's compensation (0.739%); Medicare (1.45%)—Employees hired before March 31, 1986, are exempt. In FY 2013–2014, one professional and five support staff were exempt; and Health insurance (calculated at 20.46%) billed at a flat rate of $12,029/ employee.

Question Number	Footnote

OHIO cont.

12	OhioLINK–cost factor 22.67 per FTE (total FTE 31,910). Total based on Ohio Board of Regents FY 2012–2013 report "Full-Time Equivalent Enrollment at Ohio Public Institutions in Fiscal Years 2004–2013".
14, 15	Beginning in FY 2014, approximately 150 ENG151 library instruction sessions were discontinued. This accounts for approximately 3,000 fewer participants in FY 2014.
18	OhioLINK EJC is not COUNTER but is included; also includes Springer, Highwire, Ovid, JSTOR, ScienceDirect, Cambridge, Wiley, and T&F.
19	Suspect that previous EBSCOHost numbers were incorrect causing the reason for the drop; also includes ebrary, ISI, LexisNexis, Newsbank, Ovid, JSTOR, and Elsevier (Compendex, Geobase, and ScienceDirect).
20	EBSCO only; suspect that previous numbers were incorrect.
23	2012–2013 number reported on last year's statistics in error (should have been 246). Source year correctly reported this year.
24	Previous years included only PhD programs. Added 1 AuD, 2 DPT, 1 EdD, 1 DO.
27, 29	27% increase in number of P-T Master's degree enrollment, 6.8% P-T PhD enrollment.

OHIO STATE

	Library branches included: Architecture; Biological Sciences/Pharmacy; Cartoon Research; Geology; Health Sciences; Fine Arts; Food, Agriculture ,and Environmental Sciences; Law; Ohio Agricultural Research and Development Center Library; 18th Avenue Library; Thompson (Main) Library; University Archives; Veterinary Medicine; Agricultural Technical Institute; and Regional Campus Libraries at Lima, Mansfield, Marion, and Newark.
1, 2	Recent focus on special purchases of retrospective content.
4	Intentional focus on purchasing e-books. Ramp up of Google e-book scanning project. Also includes electronic theses and dissertations.
7.a, 7.b	Higher expenditures due to spending down cash reserve.
7.c	Ackerman rental now paid under materials funding collection support.
9	Prior year included two major renovation projects.
13.a	ARL does not define "professional staff." In recent years, Libraries has included all individuals in the A&P classification. After a review of current practice, a decision was made to focus our response more narrowly. Count and FTE pulled as of 9/1 to align with ARL Salary Survey.
13.c	Student assistant count taken as of September 1, which is in line with the ARL Salary Survey and more reflective of the student assistant headcount during academic semesters.
14, 15	Focused on having greater attendance at available presentations. Although total presentations went down, total participants increased significantly.
16	Faculty retirements and issues with transaction recording influenced this change.
18	Consisted of data from COUNTER JR1 report as well as EJC downloads, which are not COUNTER compliant.
19	Number of regular searches (databases) was up approximately 4%, which can be attributed to the large number of database purchases made during the year.
20	Includes databases and platforms that provided this metric in COUNTER or platform reports (DB1, DB#, BR6, PR1). At this point only one database provides federated searches as such.
22	The CIRC numbers for requests filled for our users from other libraries INCLUDES Columbus Metro Library checkouts, which we have not included in the past. These numbers represent a significant portion (18,167) of materials provided to our users.

QUESTION NUMBER	FOOTNOTE

OHIO STATE cont.

26, 27	Large incoming freshman class including full and part-time students.

OKLAHOMA

8.a	Increase due to additional positions created and hired. [Main Library]
9	Increase expenditures resulting from one-time funds used on several small projects. [Main Library]
14	Library increased the number of Gateway courses taught in FY 2014. [Main Library]
19	The number of searches has dropped; this continues a trend we have observed over the past several years. [Main Library]
20	The decline is due to retiring the federated search interface (EBSCO EDS). [Main Library]

OKLAHOMA STATE

	Library branches included: OSU-Oklahoma City, OSU-Okmulgee, OSU-Tulsa, as well as the Architecture Library, Curriculum Materials Library, and Veterinary Medicine Library on the Stillwater campus.
	Data from the Health Sciences Library are included in the figures reported.
7.a	There was carry-forward from the previous year restricted to one-time purchases.
7.c	Changes in source of funding for collection support (OSU-OKC).
16	Previous OSU-OKC director included directional transactions in reference for FY2013. Directional transactions excluded for FY 2014.
19	The implementation of Discovery Systems is increasing the use of library databases.
20	Reduction in federated searches due to increasing use of Discovery Systems.
22	Reduction in print material requests through ILL is due to increasing availability of e-books/e-journals.

OREGON

	Library branches included: Knight (main) Library; Architecture and Allied Arts Library; Global Scholars Hall Library Commons; Mathematics Library; Rippey Library at the Oregon Institute of Marine Biology; Science Library; UO Portland Library and Learning Commons. John E. Jaqua Law Library data are included in the aggregated institutional totals in this publication, and they are also reported separately in the Law Library publication.
7, 7.a	Increased use of gift and endowment funds.
7.b	Ongoing e-book subscription added.
7.c	No longer includes ILS costs.
9	Last year's expenditure was unusually high.
10	Health care; retirement; payroll taxes; roughly 5% miscellaneous, including bus pass, worker's compensation fee, etc.
11	Health care premium cost plus 30%.
14	Fewer sessions offered.
15	More group tours.
17	Overall circulation trend is down.
19, 20	Reports from vendors vary significantly year to year.

OTTAWA

	All figures are as of 04/30/2014.

Question Number	Footnote

OTTAWA cont.

Library branches included: Main, Law, Health Sciences.

6–9, 10, 12

Expenditures as reported in Canadian dollars. Collections Expenditures: (7a) $5,973,362; (7b) $8,960,044; (7c) $11,222; (7) $14,944,628; Salary Expenditures: (8a) $4,576,456; (8b) $5,483,972; (8c) $215,419; (8) $10,275,847; (10) $2,757,359; Overall Expenditures: (7) $14,944,628; (8) $10,275,847; (9) $2,480,163; (6) $27,700,638; (12) NA/UA. NOTE: Total Salaries and Wages (Q8) EXCLUDES Fringe Benefits Expenditures (Q10).

18, 19

Selection of items for count aligns with CARL annual statistics (which counts only: CRKN, Project MUSE, PsycInfo, and Business Source Complete where COUNTER statistics are available). RESOURCES INCLUDED: Adam Matthew Digital; Alexander Street Press (includes, among other titles, Classical Music Library and Oral History Online); EBSCOhost Business Source Complete; Elsevier Scopus; Gale Cengage Learning, Eighteenth Century Collections Online; Gale Cengage Learning, Times Digital Archive; InteLex Past Masters; MathSciNet (American Mathematical Society); Micromedia ProQuest, Historical Newspapers; PsycInfo; Thomson Reuters, Web of Knowledge, Derwent Innovations Index; Thomson Reuters, Web of Knowledge, Journal Citation Reports; Thomson Reuters, Web of Knowledge, Zoological Record; Thomson Reuters, and Web of Science.

PENNSYLVANIA STATE

Library branches included: Survey includes all University Park Libraries, as well as the Campus Libraries. Campus Library locations are as follows: Abington, Altoona, Behrend, Berks, Beaver, Brandywine, DuBois, Fayette, Great Valley, Greater Allegheny, Harrisburg, Hazleton, Lehigh Valley, Mont Alto, New Kensington, Schuylkill, Shenango Valley, Wilkes-Barre, Worthington-Scranton, and York.

Data from the Law and Health Sciences Libraries are included in the figures reported.

11

Editor's Note: Published figure reflects the official designated percent for the Health Sciences Library, as this is the maximum value entered for this question.

19, 20

Due to incompatibilities within our reporting systems for electronic resources, we do not feel we can produce accurate use figures for this fiscal year. We are therefore not reporting data for lines 19 and 20.

PITTSBURGH

Library branches included: This return includes data from ULS, Law and Health Sciences libraries at the University of Pittsburgh. The University Library System (ULS) includes the Allegheny Observatory Library, Archives Service Center, African American Collection, Buhl Social Library, East Asian Collection, Frick Fine Arts Library, Hillman Library, Katz Graduate School of Business Library, Langley Library, Music Library, and the Regional Campuses of Bradford, Greensburg, Johnstown, and Titusville. The Health Sciences Library System includes the Falk Library of the Health Sciences, the UPMC Shadyside Libraries, and the Children's Hosp. Library.

4

More e-books purchased.

7.a

Shifted funds to cover costs of on-going resources.

7.b

Increasing costs of acquisitions.

9

More funds needed to cover cost of on-going resources cost.

17

This drop in circulations follows the trend over the last few years.

21, 22

FY 2012–2013 data was reported incorrectly.

23

Includes both scholarship and professional doctorates. Previous years reports only included scholarship doctorates.

Question Number	Footnote

PRINCETON

	Library branches included: East Asian, Marquand Art, Stokes Public and International Affairs, Music, Architecture, Mudd Archives, Lewis Science, Engineering, Furth Plasma Physics.
7.a	Increase due to how e-book purchases are now coded.
10	Medical expenses, employer retirement contribution, FICA taxes, other.
24	Joint degrees between academic departments have increased.

PURDUE

	Library branches included: The library system on the West Lafayette campus, consisting of 11 subject-oriented libraries, an undergraduate library, and an archives and special collections research center.
19, 20	Decrease is due to closer analysis of statistics from ProQuest database use, which have become inflated due to platform changes.

QUEEN'S

	All figures are as of 04/30/2014.
	Library branches included: Stauffer Humanities and Social Sciences, Douglas Engineering and Science, Jordan Special Collections and Music, Bracken Health Sciences, Lederman Law Library, and Education Library.
6–9, 10, 12	Expenditures as reported in Canadian dollars. Collections Expenditures: (7a) $1,090,207; (7b) $7,763,401; (7c) $698,264; (7) $9,551,872; Salary Expenditures: (8a) $4,149,817; (8b) $3,607,298; (8c) $359,527; (8) $8,116,642; (10) $1,913,875; Overall Expenditures: (7) $9,551,872; (8) $8,116,642; (9) $1,206,214; (6) $18,874,728; (12) NA/UA. NOTE: Total Salaries and Wages (Q8) EXCLUDES Fringe Benefits Expenditures (Q10).
18	This number was generated by the predefined Intota Assessment report. Queen's migrated to Intota in August 2014, and have been working with the vendor on issues with SUSHI harvesting of COUNTER statistics, so this number is known to be inaccurate but is the best information we currently have access to without reviewing statistics usage from each provider individually. A review of JR1 statistics for EBSCO, ProQuest, Elsevier, Springer, and Wiley show an 8.4% increase in full text downloads in 2013–2014 over 2012–2013.
19	This number generated by the predefined Intota Assessment report. DB1 search statistics were not properly loaded for major providers including EBSCO and ProQuest, resulting in highly inaccurate results for a DB1 search for all providers for 2013–2014. The report available to us shows 1,921,345, but when we look at a sampling of providers that did have statistics loaded, we are seeing small increases or decreases that lead us to believe that our numbers are not significantly different from those reported in 2012–2013. We will continue to work with our vendor to have statistics loaded so we can get a more accurate picture of use in 2013–2014.

RICE

	Library branches included: Fondren Library, Business Information Center.
1	Includes 24,273 Texshare e-books; 77,268 Government publication e-books; 12,483 Netlibrary and other vendor e-books, and 8,493 ETDs.
7.a	Decrease due to flat budget and implementing patron driven acquisition program (PDA).
7.b	Includes commercial binding ($38,029).
7.c	Includes binding supplies ($20,666), cataloging utilities ($167,664), ILL ($50,152), and memberships ($208,385).
8.c	Student budget cut; more work study received.
9	Normal variation in other operating expenditures.

QUESTION NUMBER	FOOTNOTE

RICE cont.

10	Fringe benefits include: group hospital and life insurance, employer's share of FICA, workers' compensation insurance, tuition waivers, retirement contributions, unemployment taxes, and short-term disability costs.
11	Percentage is for staff. Student percentage is 1.5%.
14, 15	Decrease due to preparation for renovation in areas offering instruction.
17	Decrease follows national trends.
27, 29	Increase due to shifting university practice.

ROCHESTER

	Library branches included: Eastman School of Music Sibley Library.
1	Includes Edward G. Miner (Medical) Library.
2	Does not include Edward G. Miner (Medical) Library. Decline in the number of volumes due to withdrawals from the collection.
3	387,752 print volumes determined by physical count.
4	Includes Edward G. Miner (Medical) Library. Increase in the number of e-books represents purchase of several e-book packages.
7.a	Increase due in part to the purchase of e-journal backfiles.
7.c	Decrease due to reduction in the number of journals bound.
8.c	Fewer students hired in fiscal year ending 06/30/2014.
9	Includes facilities revitalization plan expense, PL&N focus consulting, public use equipment for four years replacement cycle, and off-site facility.
11	31% for professional staff, 37.30% for support staff.
14.a	125 based on sampling.
15.a	2,500 based on sampling.
16.a	Largely based on sampling.
18	Includes Edward G. Miner (Medical) Library. Included are journals from MA Liebert, BMJ, ACS, Cambridge, IEEE, IOP, Sage, ScienceDirect, Springer, Wiley, Highwire Press, JSTOR, and Project Muse.
19	Includes Edward G. Miner (Medical) Library. Databases include CINAHL, Ovid Medline, Ovid PsycINFO, Proquest, EBSCOhost, and Gale Cengage.

RUTGERS

	Library branches included: The aggregated institution-level totals in this publication include Newark Law Library, Camden Law Library, and campuses in Camden, Newark, and New Brunswick. Rutgers Biomedical and Health Sciences (RBHS) is a newly-created campus at Rutgers, due to the integration of the University of Medicine and Dentistry of New Jersey (UMDNJ). Therefore, these figures now also include RBHS. RBHS libraries include the George F. Smith Library in Newark and the Robert Wood Johnson Library in New Brunswick.
2, 6, 7, 7.b, 13–13.b, 14–16, 25–29	Increase due to integration of the University of Medicine and Dentistry of New Jersey (UMDNJ), now known as the Rutgers Biomedical and Health Sciences (RBHS).
7.a	One time expenditures decreased due to budget cuts and more focused spending on online resources accessible to the entire university community.
7.c	Includes $74,816.85 for shipping costs and $18,457.98 for binding costs.
8–8.b	Significant increase due to merger with UMDNJ and small salary increases.

QUESTION NUMBER	FOOTNOTE

RUTGERS cont.

9	Significant decreased due to budget cuts and due to shift of funding towards collections.
10	Fringe benefits paid by staff for 8a and 8b.
18	Includes data from January 2013 to December 2013 and only from major journal packages. Does not include any data for journals outside of the major journal packages.
19	Number of regular searches 2011–2012 revised to 5,450,492. Number of regular searches 2012–2013 revised to 3,957,024. These figures are revised based on new information obtained for analyzing and gathering statistics. Includes data from January 2013 to December 2013. Totals are from consolidated database reports; although some of the resources we subscribe to do not provide statistics, this total includes all of the data for what is available.
21	Increase due to (1) CIC membership, (2) addition of the George F. Smith Library, and (3) increased efficiency of the lending process in EZ-Borrow. (1) Rutgers holdings have proven to be a welcome addition to the CIC; in fact, for FY 2014, we lent nearly 5 times more monographs than we borrowed via UBorrow, the CIC resource sharing platform. (2) Additionally, the newly integrated George F. Smith library houses a specialized collection, which is of great interest to partner libraries. (3) Finally, there has been increased efficiency in the lending process in EZ-Borrow, facilitated by the Relais system.
23, 24	Increase due to merger with UMDNJ and previous exclusion of degrees outside of PhDs.

SASKATCHEWAN

	All figures are as of 04/30/2014.
	Library branches included: Overall Library, including the following seven branches (Education & Music, Engineering, Health Sciences, Law, Murray, Science, Veterinary Medicine, and Special Collections.
	Library branches NOT included: Theological College libraries on campus that are not part of the library system.
2	A calculation error was uncovered for volumes held impacting totals for the 2013–2014 fiscal year and previous years. The calculation used determined volumes held beginning with previous year totals and taking the net total of adds plus withdrawals in the current fiscal year and then adding electronic books. Given that the previous year total for volumes held is used as the basis for future calculations, electronic books were being double counted each year. This has resulted in inflated volumes held figures. The new figure provided for 2013–2014 corrects this error in the calculation.
4	Increase reflects emphasis on electronic material.
6–9, 10, 12	Expenditures as reported in Canadian dollars. Collections Expenditures: (7a) $2,000,814; (7b) $10,092,013; (7c) $442,277; (7) $12,535,104; Salary Expenditures: (8a) $5,738,693; (8b) $3,849,057; (8c) $393,813; (8) $9,981,563; (10) $1,543,151; Overall Expenditures: (7) $12,535,104; (8) $9,981,563; (9) $1,970,756; (6) $24,487,423; (12) NA/UA. NOTE: Total Salaries and Wages (Q8) EXCLUDES Fringe Benefits Expenditures (Q10).
6, 7	Decrease due to purchase of a special collection last year ($2,052,454) not included this year.
7.a	Decision was made in 2013–2014 fiscal year to put a limit on one-time purchases.
12	No such expenditures this fiscal year.
17	Decrease reflects emphasis on electronic material resulting in decreased circulation of physical material.
18	Based on the 2013 calendar year. Includes usage for 36,152 titles.
20	University of Saskatchewan does not use a federated search engine.

SASKATCHEWAN cont.

21, 22	Decrease due to heavier reliance on electronic resources increasingly available for free or as open access on the Internet. More journals archiving older volumes and making available with current online subscriptions reducing demand for photocopies from print sources. Also due to double counting error inflating previous year's number.
23	Includes MD, DMD, JD, PhD, DVM. 2013 Academic Year.
24	Distinct count of Degree and Major. 2013 Academic Year.
25	Reported as FTE. Note that our definition includes tenured librarians (~36 FTE). Our definition also includes faculty with primarily clinical roles (~130 FTE).
26	Reported as head count. Values matched with Fall Census report. Fall 2013.
28	Reported as head count. Fall 2013. PGCL and Non-Degree are not considered as Graduate Studies.
29	Reported as head count. Fall 2013.

SOUTH CAROLINA

	Library branches included: Hollings Special Collections Library, Library Annex, Moving Image Research Collections, Music Library, and the South Caroliniana Library.
11	Editor's Note: Published figure reflects the official designated percent for the Health Sciences Library, as this is the maximum value entered for this question.

SOUTHERN CALIFORNIA

2	Increase due to increased access to electronic resources.
8.b	Decrease in salaries and wages due to reduction in number of permanent employees.
8.c	Increase due to additional service points staffed by student workers.
13.b	Increase in staff number due to hiring temporary staffing for project activity.
22	Decrease due to increased efficiency in locally filled requests.

SOUTHERN ILLINOIS

	Data from the Law and Health Sciences Library are also included in the figures reported.
1	This is an estimated calculation that does not include a significant number of uncatalogued maps, aerial photographs, and government documents.
7.c	Memberships: $308,023; Document Delivery/ILL: $97,747; Binding: $52,416; Equipment: $0.
10	Includes sick/vacation payouts, GA health insurance, FICA, retirement, worker's compensation, life insurance, unemployment insurance, health insurance, dental insurance, and vision insurance.
11	Includes FICA, retirement, worker's compensation, life insurance, unemployment insurance, health insurance, dental insurance, and vision insurance. Editor's Note: Published figure reflects the official designated percent for the Health Sciences Library, as this is the maximum value entered for this question.
16.a	No, except the circulation portion is based on sampling.
18	Includes COUNTER statistics for abstracting and indexing databases, full-text databases, and reference sources.
19	Includes COUNTER statistics from 71 journal publishers/platforms.
20	Morris Library does not use a federated search engine.

SUNY-ALBANY

	Library branches included: Dewey Graduate Library, Science Library.

QUESTION NUMBER	FOOTNOTE

SUNY-ALBANY cont.

6	Fewer one-time purchases were made in order to accommodate rising subscription costs.
7.b	Subscription costs are constantly increasing.
9	Increased spending on computer hardware and software. Increased spending on furniture and equipment.
15	More students attended instructional sessions in addition to better reporting of instructional sessions.
17	2012–2013 initial circulations should have been reported as 53,598.
18–20	Databases have changed the way they count and report usage.
21	The University Libraries joined LVIS in 2012 and we increased our overall participation in RAPID.

SUNY-BUFFALO

2	Withdrawn microfilm and HSL periodicals.
4	Suppressed records from e-book pilot removed from catalog.
18	Does not include 424k of e-book section requests.

SUNY-STONY BROOK

	Library branches included: Music, Math/Astronomy/Physics, Chemistry, Science & Engineering, Marine and Atmospheric Science Information Center.
4	Last year, our report included e-books we had cataloged plus uncatalogued e-books retrieved from our ERMS. This year, we changed to a different ERMS which has made it more difficult to separate the Main Library data from the Health Sciences Library collections. Consequently, we are only reporting for cataloged e-books. We also revised the calculation method, and are now excluding titles from Serials Solutions.
7.c	Binding $14,168; Utilities $218,152; ILL $55,803; remote storage $60,800.
8, 8.a	Due to retirements and unable to refill the positions.
8.b, 13.a, 13.b	IT staff not paid by library in 2013–2014.
9	Tech fee account budget moved out of library for 2013–2014.
12	The decrease from last year reflects decrease in state support.
14	Due to retirements, vacancies and unable to refill the positions.
15	Due to the shortage of professional staff.
16	Due to the shortage of professional staff and unable to replace the vacancies.
17	The decrease can be attributed to increase in electronic resources including e-books.
18, 19	Not available due to change in ERM vendor.
21	The decrease can be attributed to the increase in electronic resources.
22	The decrease can be attributed to the availability of electronic resources, including e-books.
23	Doctor's degree-research/scholarship: 301; Doctor's degree-professional practice: 275; Total=576
23–39	Data for Q23-Q29 are for the whole Stony Brook University, including Health Science Library.
25	Last year we used Common Data Set definition and the number was 997. After reviewing the definition (US Education Department), our last year number should be 1,246 and this year number for full time instructional faculty is 1,332. Also, Stony Brook University has an initiative to hire more faculty. Therefore, there will be an increase in our faculty numbers.

Question Number	Footnote

SYRACUSE

	Library branches included: Carnegie, Geology, Facility.
2	Modifications to bibliographic count processes.
4	From Serials Solutions Data Summary. These titles will be included in MARC Updates for e-books and reflected in catalog.
8.a, 8.b	Changes in how staff were classified for ARL reporting purposes, e.g., non-MLSs in librarian positions, who are support staff. They are now based on level instead of title, which are in the midst of changing based on standardization within the university.
11	Reflects the official percentage for professional staff only.
13.a	Changes in how staff were classified for ARL reporting purposes, e.g., non-MLSs in librarian positions, who is support staff..
13.c	Reductions in work-study funds available.
16	Data drawn from "New Metrics PatronAssist" tab of PatronAssistance.xlsx file in PMC Docs operational metrics folder. Includes Reference, Print Access, Electronic Access. Does not include "Directional" or "Tech Support" based on ARL definition.
18	Fiscal Year: 2014. Source: COUNTER Reports JR1 and JR2 Reporting data updated 9/23. 930,436 + 2,888 from JR1a (archived) = 933,324.
19	Source: COUNTER Reports DB1 and DB2. Month: July 2013 to June 2014. No rational explanation for last year's value beyond data entry error.
20	Source: COUNTER Reports DB1 and DB2. Month: July 2013 to June 2014.
21	Significant improvements in ability to respond to ILL requests from other libraries, including workflow automations.
23	Numbers are supplied by the university's Office of Research (OIRA), and have been verified as correct.

TEMPLE

	Library branches included: Ginsburg Health Sciences Library, Beasley Law Library, and Special Collections Research Center.
11	Editor's Note: Published figure reflects the official designated percent for the Law Library, as this is the maximum value entered for this question.
18–19	Figure based on 2013 calendar year.

TENNESSEE

	Library branches included: UT Libraries-Knoxville (Hodges [Main] Library, Pendergrass Agriculture and Veterinary Medicine Library, Devine Music Library, Social Work Library, and UT Space Institute Library. Data from the Law Library and the Health Science Libraries are also included in the figures reported.

TEXAS

	All figures are as of 08/31/2014.
	Library branches included: University of Texas at Austin Libraries, the Briscoe Center for American History, the Tarlton Law Library, and the Harry Ransom Center.
2	The volume count includes e-books such as EBL, MyILibrary, ebrary, Gale Virtual Reference, ARTFL, CIAO, LION, Evans Early American Imprints, Making of Modern Law, Sabin Americana, Making of America, Oxford Reference-books online, Gerritsen, History e-book (now Humanities), OECD, World Bank eLibrary, Annual Reviews, Si Ku Quan Shu, Old English Corpus, Heritage Quest, Stat Reference, Thesaurus Linguae Graecae, and CHANT–Chinese Ancient Texts.

QUESTION NUMBER	FOOTNOTE

TEXAS cont.

7	Includes total expenditures for library materials of $20,922,649 by the University Libraries, $1,531,673 by the Tarlton Law Library, and $3,324,864 by the Harry Ransom Humanities Research Center.
8.c	Includes federal work-study funds.
9	In May 2014, our provost approved and funded a Learning Commons project in the Perry Castaneda Library. We have a $4M budget that will be used to relocate Technical Services staff from 20,000 sq. ft. on the entry level down to the first floor, and then we will design and build a Learning Commons that will include active learning classrooms, a large digital media lab, and the campus writing center. Project completion 08/2015.
11	32% is the official designated percent for salaried staff. 8.4% is the official designated percent for wage staff.
16.a	There is a mixture of sampling and non-sampling that was used to generate this figure.
18, 19	We counted statistics for July 2013 to June 2014 because this was the most current full year of statistics available to us through our statistics tool, 360 Counter, due to the tool's biannual upload schedule.
19	For providers that offered both DB1 and DB3/PR1 reports, we chose to include only the DB3/PR1 report in the total in order to avoid duplicate counting. For providers that only offered one type of database report, we used whichever report was available. The number of searches is significantly lower than what we reported last year due to an error in including EBSCO statistics for all UT System schools last year rather than for UT Austin only.
20	For this question, we counted the number of searches in our discovery tool, Summon, for August 2013 to July 2014. Statistics in this tool are continually updated, so we did not have to shift the months reported like we did in the previous two questions.

TEXAS A&M

	All figures are as of 08/31/2014.
	Library branches included: Cushing Memorial Library and Archives, Dee J. Kelly Law Library, Jack K. Williams Library (Galveston), Library Annex, Map and GIS Library, Medical Sciences Library Bryan, Medical Sciences Library College Station, Medical Sciences Library Kingsville, Medical Sciences Library Round Rock, Medical Sciences Library Temple, Policy Sciences and Economics Library (PSEL), Sterling C. Evans Library, Technical Reference Center (Architecture Library), Texas A&M University at Qatar Library, West Campus Library, and Joint Library Facility.
2, 8.b, 13.b	First year that the University Libraries is including a full data set for the Dee J. Kelly Law Library. The increase reflects this additional resources.
11	Support for fringe benefits for Texas A&M University Libraries employees has come from various university and system funds over the course of the past few years. As a result, there has been and will continue to be a difference between the official fringe benefit percentage stipulated and the actual fringe benefit percentage paid out. With recent merger and reorganization activity that has occurred and is occurring at the university and system levels this more than likely will continue through at least one more fiscal year.
21, 22	Decrease reflects growing increase in accessing materials through online providers rather than directly from a library.
23	As part of Texas A&M University's merger with the Texas A&M Health Science Center and acquisition of the law school, several degree programs came under review. That process is continuing and expected to result in significant variances for a number of years. (This is especially the case as the newly organized university prepares for SACSCOC re-certification in 2016).

QUESTION NUMBER	FOOTNOTE

TEXAS A&M cont.

25, 28, 29	Increase reflects the acquisition of a law school into the Texas A&M University umbrella.
27	At the same time enrollment has increased because of the acquisition of the law school, the university has continued programs to reduce part-time enrollment and promote full-time four year programs.

TEXAS TECH

	All figures are as of 08/31/2014.
	Library branches included: Southwest Collections/Special Collections Library, Vietnam Archive, Education, Museum, and the Architecture Library.
1	Represents Southwest Collection/Special Collections Library only.
10	Includes worker's compensation insurance, health match, TRS matching, ORP matching, opt out health matching, lump sum vacation pool, retiree insurance pool, Medicaid, Medicare, FICA, and social security.
11	Editor's Note: Published figure reflects the official designated percent for the Health Sciences Library, as this is the maximum value entered for this question.
16	Increase due to the way Southwest Collections/Special Collections were counting transactions. None of their items circulate so previous year's numbers should have been reflected in reference transactions but were incorrectly counted as circulation transactions.
17	Decrease due to the way Southwest Collections/Special Collections were counting transactions. None of their items circulate so numbers should have been reflected in reference transactions.
19	Vietnam Archives increased 4,818,679, the Southwest Collection/Special Collection Library increased 323,913, while the University Library increased 2,046,736.
20	Problems were corrected to enable a full year count.
23	Law degrees were not included in previous years reporting, the error has been corrected for this reporting cycle. The number reported for this fiscal year is preliminary.
24	Law degrees were not included in previous years reporting.

TORONTO

	All figures are as of 04/30/2014.
	Library branches included: All 44 libraries in the U of T Library system.
6–9, 10, 12	Expenditures as reported in Canadian dollars. Collections Expenditures: (7a) $13,830,732; (7b) $17,485,101; (7c) $507,417; (7) $31,823,250; Salary Expenditures: (8a) $17,114,695; (8b) $18,638,242; (8c) $4,443,067; (8) $40,196,004; (10) $9,517,256; Overall Expenditures: (7) $31,823,250; (8) $40,196,004; (9) $14,508,617; (6) $86,527,871; (12) NA/UA. NOTE: Total Salaries and Wages (Q8) EXCLUDES Fringe Benefits Expenditures (Q10).
7.a	Includes dedicated gift and grant funds used for a one-time special purchase.
9	In 2012–2013, the operating expenditures of one large library branch were not included in the reported figure. For 2013–2014, this figure includes a major one-time equipment purchase funded by a provincial government grant.
14	Number of sessions reported in 2012–2013 was incorrect. It should have been 2,400.
25	Decrease in FT faculty is due to increase in sessional contract faculty.

TULANE

	Library branches included: Figures with the main (Howard-Tilton) library include those from the Turchin Business Library and the Vorhoff Library at the Newcomb Center for Research on Women. Also Tulane's Architecture Library, Math Library, and the Amistad Research Center.

QUESTION NUMBER	FOOTNOTE

TULANE cont.

1	Increase due to retrospective cataloging and bulk loading of records for digital sets.
7.a	Increase primarily related to purchase of digital historical collections and some new rare print titles.
8.c	Decrease due to decline in student budget.
9	Decrease due to fewer capital purchases (furniture, projects, etc.)
14–15, 17	Decrease may have been influenced by disruption from ongoing library construction.
18	Decrease may reflect increase in discoverability of other kinds of resources.
19, 20	Effect of library website redesign.
23–26, 28, 29	Increase may reflect a mix of institutional growth and changes to how these numbers are counted by the university's Office of Institutional Research.

UTAH

11	Fringe benefits for faculty and staff is 42% and 8% for hourly student employees.
18	Previous years did not count full-text article requests paid for with consortial funding.
24	We suspect an error in previous years reporting for this question. This year's figure was captured directly from the university's Office of Budget and Institutional Analysis.

VANDERBILT

	Library branches included: Central, Divinity, Peabody, Management, Music, Science & Engineering.
1, 2, 4	Major e-book collections added in FY 2013–2014: EBSCO E-books Academic Collection, updates to Eighteenth Century Collections Online, additions to Academic Complete, and other smaller collections.
7.a	Decrease due to need to cover increases in ongoing resource purchases.
10	Includes health plan, life insurance, disability insurance, retirement plan, tuition assistance, vacation and sick leave.
13	Includes Dean's Fellows. Should have been 162 last year.
13.a	Should have been 75 professional staff last year. Decrease due to unfilled vacancies.
13.b	Includes new Dean's Fellow Positions. Should have been 69 support staff last year.
13.c	Should have been 18 students last year.
16	Lacking data from one library in 2012–2013: number should have been 13,257.
18, 19	Better counting mechanism.
20	Students prefer discovery layer instead of federated search.
23	Included 20 Nursing DNP's last year.

VIRGINIA

	Library branches included: Astronomy, Brown Science and Engineering, Chemistry, Clemons, Education, Fine Arts, Math, Music, Physics, and Ivy. [University Library]
1	This year, we included titles for our digital collections. These titles are not countable in our SIRSI counts (the title counts used for past years). The digital collections titles are available in our public catalog. [University Library]
18	The figure given is for all article requests, including Darden, Health, Law, and Special Collections. They all share the same public interface. [University Library]
20	We do not track federated searches. [University Library]

QUESTION NUMBER	FOOTNOTE

VIRGINIA cont.

24	Data corrected to match that reported by State Council of Higher Education of Virginia. Previous years had been manual count from Programs and Degrees Offered on the website of the University Registrar. [University Library]

VIRGINIA TECH

	Library branches included: Carilion, WAAC (employees and partial collections), NOVA, Art n Architecture, Vet Med, Storage, and Warehouse (and Special Collections).
1	Increase due to cataloging previously uncatalogued materials and an e-book package purchase.
4	Purchase of a large e-book package.
10	Fringe benefits include educational leave, faculty/staff fee waiver, workers compensation, unemployment compensation, employer retirement contribution, retiree health insurance benefits, FICA, group life, medical-hospitalization, VA Sickness and Disability Program, TSA–Employer Cash Match, and WTA-Workforce Transition Benefits.
22	Purchase on Demand allows us to buy articles and books that we cannot obtain from other lenders, and in the past we had to cancel the requests. Also, with increased use of Summon, patrons request articles via the Get VText page more readily. Finally, there are just more people requesting things.

WASHINGTON

	Library branches included: University of Washington Bothell and University of Washington Tacoma, Law, and Health Sciences. [Main Library]
1	Number of titles not available due to system migration. [Main Library]
10	Fringe benefits include retirement system premiums, health insurance plans, Medicare, Social Security, unemployment, and medical aid contributions. [Main Library]
11	Benefit rates vary according to employee group: Librarians and professional staff 30.9%, classified staff 35.3%, and students at 15.2%. [Main Library]
19	Estimated total. [Main Library]

WASHINGTON STATE

	Library branches included: WSU-Vancouver, WSU-Tri-Cities, WSU Energy Library, and WSU Riverpoint Campus Library.
1	The figure probably overstates our true holdings. We installed a new integrated library system halfway through the fiscal year, and have not yet mastered deduplication in reports, nor finished cleaning up the data transferred from the old system.
4	The increase from the preceding year's figure is partly due to a backlog of e-book records being entered into our new ILS as part of the system transition.
7.c	Credits recovered on collections support funds make the actual expenditure negative (-$12,254). Because the reporting interface will not accept negative entries, these credits have been applied to one-time library materials expenditures in this report. The actual figures are as follows: One-time expenditures: $571,274; on-going expenditures: $6,288,664; collection support: -$12,254.
10	Includes OASI, retirement, and insurance.
11	Percentage varies by department and employment type.
19	The number of searches is inflated by an unknown amount due to the inclusion of certain databases in the default search of our discovery layer. Data is reported for databases on the following platforms: Communication Institute for Online Scholarship, CQ Press, CRC Press LLC, EBSCOhost, Gale, Greenwood Publishing Group, IBISWorld, IGI Global, Lexi-Comp, OCLC, Ovid, Project MUSE, ProQuest, and Thomson Reuters.

WASHINGTON STATE cont.

22	It was discovered that some ILL transactions were double-counted in previous years. The correct figure for 2012–2013 is 38,976.

WASHINGTON U.-ST. LOUIS

7	Reflects law library acquisition budget cuts.
10	Fringe benefits include annuity, FICA, health allowance, and dependent tuition allowance.
22	High percent change since last year reflects 2013 law library reporting error due to inaccurate count of patron-initiated requests to libraries in the statewide MOBIUS Library Consortium and completion last year of law faculty project which made heavy use of ILL.
24–29	Includes numbers for all branches.
24	Incorrect input for last year; should be 47 instead of 55. That revised number would yield a variance of -10.6%.

WATERLOO

	All figures are as of 04/30/2014.
	Library branches included: Dana Porter, Davis Centre, Witer Resource Centre, Musagetes Architecture, Pharmacy, and the Annex off-site storage.
1	Previous year did not report different formats as separate titles.
6–9, 10, 12	Expenditures as reported in Canadian dollars. Collections Expenditures: (7a) $962,467; (7b) $8,219,097; (7c) $308,536; (7) $9,490,100; Salary Expenditures: (8a) $2,884,461; (8b) $4,164,576; (8c) $886,596; (8) $7,935,633; (10) $1,760,845; Overall Expenditures: (7) $9,490,100; (8) $7,935,633; (9) $1,688,810; (6) $19,114,543; (12) NA/UA. NOTE: Total Salaries and Wages (Q8) EXCLUDES Fringe Benefits Expenditures (Q10).
11	18–24% depending on whether they have single or family benefits. The median for professional librarians, 21%, is reported here.
13.a	Professional staff FTE includes one staff seconded from elsewhere on campus, and three librarians working on temporary contracts.
19	As last year, the Primo Central search statistics used for calendar 2013 reflect only part of actual use (only searches starting from the 'Articles+' tab on the library's search page); combined Primo/Primo Central searches beginning from the 'Search' tab are not included. For this reason, actual total database searches would be considerably higher than the figure shown.

WAYNE STATE

	All figures are as of 9/30/2014.
	Library branches included: The Reuther Archives of Labor and Urban Affairs, the Shiffman Medical Library, and the Neef Law Library. The medical and law library statistics cannot be disaggregated from the main statistics because the medical and law collections are an integral part of the main library.
1, 2	The Reuther Archives of Labor and Urban Affairs (WSU's Special Collections Branch) reported neither volumes nor titles in 2013–2014.
6	These expenditures include $826,794 from the Reuther Archives of Labor and Urban Affairs (WSU's Special Collections Branch).
7	There were no library material expenditures by the Reuther Archives of Labor and Urban Affairs (WSU's Special Collections Branch) in 2013–2014.
7.c	Collection Support is the sum of our expenditures on Bibliographic Utilities, Networks, and Consortia ($98,547), contract binding ($14,080), and document delivery/ILL ($105,615).

WAYNE STATE cont.

8   This total includes $749,632 in salaries and wages from the Reuther Archives of Labor and Urban Affairs (WSU's Special Collections Branch).

8.a   These salaries and wages contain $704,621 from the Reuther Archives of Labor and Urban Affairs (WSU's Special Collections Branch).

8.b   These salaries and wages contain $5,239 from the Reuther Archives of Labor and Urban Affairs (WSU's Special Collections Branch).

8.c   These salaries and wages contain $39,772 from the Reuther Archives of Labor and Urban Affairs (WSU's Special Collections Branch).

9   These expenditures include $77,162 from the Reuther Archives of Labor and Urban Affairs (WSU's Special Collections Branch).

10   Fringe benefits are not paid from the libraries' budgets. This estimate includes $189,987 in fringe benefits paid to the staff of the Reuther Archives of Labor and Urban Affairs (WSU's Special Collections Branch).

11   Fringe benefits for both professional and support staff positions are officially designated to be 26.8%. Benefits for student assistants and temporary and part-time staff are calculated at much lower percentages.

13   This total contains 17 position from the Reuther Archives of Labor and Urban Affairs (WSU's Special Collections Branch).

13.a   This total contains 11 positions from the Reuther Archives of Labor and Urban Affairs (WSU's Special Collections Branch).

13.b   This total contains 2 positions from the Reuther Archives of Labor and Urban Affairs (WSU's Special Collections Branch).

13.c   This total contains 4 positions from the Reuther Archives of Labor and Urban Affairs (WSU's Special Collections Branch).

14–16   No data from the Reuther Archives of Labor and Urban Affairs (WSU's Special Collections Branch) were reported in 2013–2014.

18   This figure is based on reports for 48,099 resources.

WESTERN

                 All figures are as of 04/30/2014.

                 Library branches included: Archives and Research Collections Centre, C.B. "Bud" Johnston Library (Business), Education Library, John & Dotsa Bitove Family Law Library, Music Library, Allyn & Betty Taylor Library, The D.B. Weldon Library, and Map & Data Centre.

6–9, 10, 12   Expenditures as reported in Canadian dollars. Collections Expenditures: (7a) $1,878,300; (7b) $11,630,380; (7c) $719,406; (7) $14,228,086; Salary Expenditures: (8a) $5,296,200; (8b) $4,091,763; (8c) $248,317; (8) $9,636,280; (10) $2,556,817; Overall Expenditures: (7) $14,228,086; (8) $9,636,280; (9) $2,110,099; (6) $25,974,465; (12) NA/UA. NOTE: Total Salaries and Wages (Q8) EXCLUDES Fringe Benefits Expenditures (Q10).

7.b   Increase due to increases in ongoing resource costs.

7.c   Includes binding, memberships, bibliographic utilities, access, software. Increased amount in 2012–2013 was partly due to purchase of software to support ILS and collections decisions, as well as off-site storage.

8.c   Changes in staffing levels.

9   Increase due to construction, renovation, and furnishing costs.

QUESTION NUMBER	FOOTNOTE

WESTERN cont.

11	Included was the actual benefit costs to Western Libraries. Western Libraries is charged benefits at a rate of 27.5% for all full-time permanent employees. Western Libraries is charged at a rate of 13% for student assistants and contract support staff.
14	36 of these presentations were online.
15	1,738 of these participants were in online presentations.
17	Decrease could be attributed to multiple factors, including increase of e-book usage.
18–20	Unavailable. Western Libraries has purchased software to assist in collecting usage data and hopes to be able to contribute this data in future surveys.
22	Fewer interlibrary loan requests from Western students/staff/faculty.
29	Fairly consistent 10% decrease across faculties in part-time enrollment.

WISCONSIN

	Library branches included: Main (GLS) (General Library System): Archives, Art, Astronomy, Business, Chemistry, Undergraduate, Geography, Geology & Geophysics, Math, Memorial, Music, Physics, School of Library & Information Science (SLIS), Social Science, Social Work, Space Science, Special Collections, Steenbock (agriculture & life sciences), and Wendt (engineering). Affiliate libraries: Cooperative Children's Book Center (CCBC), Education (MERIT), Health (Ebling), Law, Map, and Wisconsin Historical Society (American history).
	Library branches NOT included: African American Studies, American Indian Studies Program, Arboretum, Center for Demography & Ecology, Chicano & Latino Studies, Journalism Reading Room, Max Kade German-American Institute, Limnology Reading Room, Learning Support Services, Morgridge Center Library, Trout Lake Collection, University Communications Library, and the Wisconsin's Water Library.
4	This reported figure represents the UW Madison campus-wide total for electronic books.
7.c	Includes postage, bindery expenditures (external), and additional funding for CIC. Represents Main library, including SLIS (library school), Memorial (humanities and social sciences), Steenbock (agricultural and life sciences), and Wendt (engineering) libraries.
8	Staff figures include staff working for a learning collaborative WisCEL but funded by College of Engineering in support of Wendt Engineering Library. The Main (GLS) library also includes WisCEL staff however funded by GLS/Main library funding specifically.
12	According to the University of Wisconsin System source, in FY2014 expenditures for Share Electronic Collections included up-front payments of five-year subscriptions for ACS, IEEE, Wiley e-book packages, and WorlCat subscriptions. The reported expenditures is specific to UW-Madison. FY2015 expenditures should be significantly less.
13, 13.c	There is a significant decline in the reported FTEs for student assistants compared to previous ARL annual reports. Previous data submissions did not calculate actual FTEs for student assistants for Main (GLS) libraries.
15	Presentation by Cooperative Children's Book Center (CCBC) to classes from UW-Madison campus include 17 on-site presentations totaling 245 students. Presentations to librarians/teachers visiting the CCBC included eight on-site presentations to groups totaling 107 individuals. These eight presentations include presentations to educators from CESA #5, Lake Mills School District, Madison Metropolitan School District, and early childhood educators from UW-Platteville and Orchard Ridge Nursery School in Madison. Outreach Presentations to Librarians/Teachers around WI included 12 presentations and workshops around the state totaling 127 individuals. Also included in CCBC's data, numerous presentation and exhibits statewide, as well as distance programming via webinars.
16	The reported figure represents a sample and includes ICONS held campus-wide.

QUESTION NUMBER	FOOTNOTE

WISCONSIN cont.

18 Numbers are not comprehensive, but do include aggregators and individual journal titles/packages using COUNTER JR1 report.

19 Numbers are not comprehensive, but consist of databases using COUNTER R3 report and de-duped where possible.

20 Metalib stats are prorated to cover full year + Primo stats.

21 2013–2014 we used a different method to capture the data.

YALE

Library branches included: Haas Arts Library, Bass, Beinecke, Center for Science & Social Science Information (CSSSI), Classics, Divinity, Geology, Law, Lewis Walpole, Mathematics, Medical, Music, Sterling Memorial Library, and Library Shelving Facility (LSF).

Library branches NOT included: Residential College Libraries and Museum Libraries (Yale Art, Yale Center for British Art).

1 The methodology used to gather data changed for FY 2014.

2 The methodology used to gather data changed for FY 2014. Represents total number of items in the YUL system with item records in the Yale University Library catalog. There are segments of the collection on campus that are not completely barcoded and identified in the system.

4 Represents e-books for all collections; due to the way electronic resources are managed at Yale, we cannot identify law and medical e-books as separate counts.

7.a, 7.b Change in reporting methodology.

11 Salaried/professional range: 29.4%–32.6%; Hourly/support range: 53.6%–54.6%.

12 Consortia–State of Connecticut.

16.a Yale Medical Library uses sampling to track reference transactions.

YORK

All figures are as of 04/30/2014.

Library branches included: Bronfman Business Library, Frost Library, Scott Library, and the Steacie Science & Engineering Library.

4 Total consists of MARC records in SIRSI (727,512) and Scholars Portal Public Collection e-books (404,723).

6–9, 10, 12 Expenditures as reported in Canadian dollars. Collections Expenditures: (7a) $3,335,483; (7b) $8,328,382; (7c) $107,790; (7) $11,771,655; Salary Expenditures: (8a) $7,420,188; (8b) $5,349,374; (8c) $1,007,843; (8) $13,777,405; (10) $3,004,418; Overall Expenditures: (7) $11,771,655; (8) $13,777,405; (9) $1,906,814; (6) $27,455,874; (12) NA/UA. NOTE: Total Salaries and Wages (Q8) EXCLUDES Fringe Benefits Expenditures (Q10).

7.a Reduced purchasing in this area resulting from fewer year-end OTO purchasing funds being available in 2013–2014.

11 Official designated percent: Faculty 20%; other professionals 22 %; staff 27.5%; casuals 10%.

17 Last year's figure should have been 284,920.

BOSTON PUBLIC LIBRARY

Library branches included: 24 Branches.

NATIONAL RESEARCH COUNCIL CANADA

Due to capacity issues, note that the 2013–2014 reported data are the same as the 2012–2013 data.

NATIONAL RESEARCH COUNCIL CANADA cont.

6–9, 10, 12

Expenditures as reported in Canadian dollars. Collections Expenditures: (7a) NA/UA; (7b) NA/UA; (7c) NA/UA; (7) NA/UA; Salary Expenditures: (8a) NA/UA; (8b) NA/UA; (8c) NA/UA; (8) NA/UA; (10) NA/UA; Overall Expenditures: (7) NA/UA; (8) NA/UA; (9) NA/UA; (6) $18,626,053; (12) NA/UA. NOTE: Total Salaries and Wages (Q8) EXCLUDES Fringe Benefits Expenditures (Q10).

CENTER FOR RESEARCH LIBRARIES

7.b

This includes both one-time and ongoing expenditures.

10

Fringe benefits include FICA, worker's compensation, and all other benefits.

LIBRARY OF CONGRESS

All figures are as of 09/30/2014.

Library branches included: Law Library of Congress, Library Services.

Library branches NOT included: National Library Service for the Blind and Physically Handicapped, Congressional Research Service (except where noted), and the US Copyright Office.

Many statistics reported for fiscal 2014 are lower than the same statistics for the previous year, mainly because in 2014 the Library of Congress was closed from October 1–16 because of the partial federal government shutdown and for an additional five days because of inclement weather.

2

Includes an estimated 150,118 standard manuscript containers. A standard manuscript container, or circulation unit, holds 350 manuscript sheets on average. Does not include manuscripts in uncatalogued arrearage. Also includes 1,041,000 e-monographs and e-serials, cataloged in LC Electronic Resources Online Catalog and accessible to patrons on-site.

4

Includes 886,000 distinct monograph and serial titles. All are cataloged in LC Electronic Resources Online Catalog and can be accessed by patrons on-site.

7.b

Includes $4,614,853 for subscriptions and $4,837,064 for licensed e-resources.

10

Includes set-aside funds for workers' compensation and federal transportation subsidy for mass transit commuters; federal group life insurance plans; hardship post pay, etc.; and government contributions, administered in the US Office of Personnel Management, to employee retirement plans.

11

Estimated; exact figures are not possible, because most federal fringe benefits are administered by the US Office of Personnel Management or other federal agencies external to the Library of Congress. The estimate of 30 percent applies to employees covered by the Federal Employee Retirement System, who now are about 75 percent of library staff.

14

Number of presentations to groups declined from previous year because in fiscal 2104 LC public service divisions were closed to the public 19 days (14 days by partial government shutdown, 5 days by weather). Does not include webinars or remote learning opportunities.

15

Does not include webinar or remote learning participants.

16

Does not include 593,000 congressional reference requests or reference service at National Library Service for the Blind and Physically Handicapped. Number of reference inquiries declined from previous year. In fiscal 2104, LC public service divisions were closed to the public 19 days (14 days by partial government shutdown, 5 days by weather).

17

Does not include 23 million items circulated by the National Library Service for the Blind and Physically Handicapped or 20,600 volumes circulated to congressional offices.

20

Includes searches of all Library of Congress web properties.

QUESTION NUMBER	FOOTNOTE

NATIONAL AGRICULTURAL LIBRARY

All figures are as of 09/30/2014.

NATIONAL ARCHIVES

All figures are as of 09/30/2014.

9 — 2012–2013 entry was an entry error. Correct number should be 172,584,550.

14 — PMRS Education Statistics All Programs.

NATIONAL LIBRARY OF MEDICINE

All figures are as of 09/30/2014.

7 — Decreased significantly due to the SWETS bankruptcy, which caused NLM to delay major collections expenditures.

7.a — Memberships, monographs, AVs, and backfiles of serials.

7.b — Decreased significantly due to the SWETS bankruptcy, which caused NLM to delay major collections expenditures. NLM anticipates that expenditures will increase in FY2015 to compensate for the FY2014 decrease.

7.c — $724,354 for Binding, Binding Prep, and Shelving (increased to reduce backlog created by previous budget cuts), $55,510 for OCLC Bibliographic Utility, and $10,243 for Security Labels.

10 — Includes employer share of taxes, health and life insurance, and retirement.

11 — There is no official percentage amount for US Federal employees as the amount depends on the employee's type of appointment to the Federal Civil Service and the benefits they select. NLM has provided an average benefit percentage amount.

18 — NLM does not have COUNTER-compliant usage statistics data available.

NEW YORK PUBLIC LIBRARY

6 — Figure includes multi-year payments.

SMITHSONIAN

National Air and Space Museum Library, Washington, DC; National Museum of American History, Washington, DC; National Museum of Natural History Library, Washington, DC; National Postal Museum Library, Washington, DC; National Zoological Park Library, Washington, DC; Smithsonian American Art Museum, National Portrait Gallery Library, Washington, DC; Smithsonian Environmental Research Center Library, Edgewater, Maryland; Anacostia Museum and Center for African American History and Culture Library, Washington, DC; Botany and Horticulture Library, Washington, DC; Cooper-Hewitt National Design Museum Library, New York, New York; Dibner Library of the History of Science and Technology, Washington, DC; Earl S. Tupper Library Smithsonian Tropical Research Institute, Republic of Panama; Freer Gallery of Art and Arthur M. Sackler Gallery Library, Washington, DC; Hirshhorn Museum and Sculpture Garden Library, Washington, DC; John Wesley Powell Library of Anthropology, Washington, DC; Joseph F. Cullman, 3rd Library of Natural History, Washington, DC; Museum Studies and Reference Library, Washington, DC; Museum Support Center Library, Suitland, Maryland; Vine Deloria Jr. Library, National Museum of the American Indian, Suitland, Maryland; and Warren M. Robbins Library, National Museum of African Art, Washington DC.)

6 — Private funding increased allowing more spending on digitization. We also filled several positions that had been vacant due to buyouts in previous years.

7.a — Due to increase in private donations and endowment payout, were able to spend more on book purchases.

9 — Due to increase in private funding we spent more on digitization efforts.

14 — There were fewer presentations, but larger audiences for them.

QUESTION NUMBER	FOOTNOTE

SMITHSONIAN cont.

16, 17	We suspect that user access to online resources is causing drop in requests for reference and in the borrowing of materials.
19	Source of data has changed.
20	We now use ProQuest's Summon product, which we call "One Search" to pull search responses from multiple platforms.

ARL Member Libraries as of January 1, 2014

The Association of Research Libraries (ARL) represents the interests of 125 libraries that serve major North American research institutions. The ARL Statistics and Measurement program is organized around identifying, collecting, analyzing, and distributing quantifiable information describing the characteristics of research libraries.

Institution	Category	Full Name of Institution	Location
Alabama	S	University of Alabama	Tuscaloosa, Alabama
Alberta	C	University of Alberta	Edmonton, Alberta
Arizona	S	University of Arizona	Tucson, Arizona
Arizona State	S	Arizona State University	Tempe, Arizona
Auburn	S	Auburn University	Auburn, Alabama
Boston	P	Boston University	Boston, Massachusetts
Boston College	P	Boston College	Boston, Massachusetts
Brigham Young	P	Brigham Young University	Provo, Utah
British Columbia	C	University of British Columbia	Vancouver, British Columbia
Brown	P	Brown University	Providence, Rhode Island
Berkeley, California	S	University of California, Berkeley	California, Berkeley
Calgary	C	University of Calgary	Calgary, Alberta
California, Davis	S	University of California, Davis	Davis, California
California, Irvine	S	University of California, Irvine	Irvine, California
California, Los Angeles	S	University of California, Los Angeles	Los Angeles, California
California, Riverside	S	University of California, Riverside	Riverside, California
California, San Diego	S	University of California, San Diego	La Jolla, California
California, Santa Barbara	S	University of California, Santa Barbara	Santa Barbara, California
Case Western Reserve	P	Case Western Reserve University	Cleveland, Ohio
Chicago	P	University of Chicago	Chicago, Illinois
Cincinnati	S	University of Cincinnati	Cincinnati, Ohio
Colorado	S	University of Colorado	Boulder, Colorado
Colorado State	S	Colorado State University	Fort Collins, Colorado
Columbia	P	Columbia University	New York, New York
Connecticut	S	University of Connecticut	Storrs, Connecticut
Cornell	P	Cornell University	Ithaca, New York
Dartmouth	P	Dartmouth College	Hanover, New Hampshire
Delaware	S	University of Delaware	Newark, Delaware
Duke	P	Duke University	Durham, North Carolina
Emory	P	Emory University	Atlanta, Georgia
Florida	S	University of Florida	Gainesville, Florida
Florida State	S	Florida State University	Tallahassee, Florida
George Washington	P	George Washington University	Washington, DC
Georgetown	P	Georgetown University	Washington, DC
Georgia	S	University of Georgia	Athens, Georgia
Georgia Tech	S	Georgia Institute of Technology	Atlanta, Georgia
Guelph	C	University of Guelph	Guelph, Ontario
Harvard	P	Harvard University	Cambridge, Massachusetts
Hawaii	S	University of Hawaii	Honolulu, Hawaii

Institution	Category	Full Name of Institution	Location
Houston	S	University of Houston	Houston, Texas
Howard	P	Howard University	Washington, DC
Illinois, Chicago	S	University of Illinois at Chicago	Chicago, Illinois
Illinois, Urbana	S	University of Illinois at Urbana-Champaign	Urbana, Illinois
Indiana	S	Indiana University	Bloomington, Indiana
Iowa	S	University of Iowa	Iowa City, Iowa
Iowa State	S	Iowa State University	Ames, Iowa
Johns Hopkins	P	Johns Hopkins University	Baltimore, Maryland
Kansas	S	University of Kansas	Lawrence, Kansas
Kent State	S	Kent State University	Kent, Ohio
Kentucky	S	University of Kentucky	Lexington, Kentucky
Laval	C	Laval University	Quebec, Quebec
Louisiana State	S	Louisiana State University	Baton Rouge, Louisiana
Louisville	S	University of Louisville	Louisville, Kentucky
McGill	C	McGill University	Montreal, Quebec
McMaster	C	McMaster University	Hamilton, Ontario
Manitoba	C	University of Manitoba	Winnipeg, Manitoba
Maryland	S	University of Maryland	College Park, Maryland
Massachusetts	S	University of Massachusetts	Amherst, Massachusetts
MIT	P	Massachusetts Institute of Technology	Cambridge, Massachusetts
Miami	P	University of Miami	Coral Gables, Florida
Michigan	S	University of Michigan	Ann Arbor, Michigan
Michigan State	S	Michigan State University	East Lansing, Michigan
Minnesota	S	University of Minnesota	Minneapolis, Minnesota
Missouri	S	University of Missouri	Columbia, Missouri
Montreal	C	University of Montreal	Montreal, Quebec
Nebraska	S	University of Nebraska-Lincoln	Lincoln, Nebraska
New Mexico	S	University of New Mexico	Albuquerque, New Mexico
New York	P	New York University	New York, New York
North Carolina	S	University of North Carolina	Chapel Hill, North Carolina
North Carolina State	S	North Carolina State University	Raleigh, North Carolina
Northwestern	P	Northwestern University	Evanston, Illinois
Notre Dame	P	University of Notre Dame	Notre Dame, Indiana
Ohio	S	Ohio University	Athens, Ohio
Ohio State	S	Ohio State University	Columbus, Ohio
Oklahoma	S	University of Oklahoma	Norman, Oklahoma
Oklahoma State	S	Oklahoma State University	Stillwater, Oklahoma
Oregon	S	University of Oregon	Eugene, Oregon
Ottawa	C	University of Ottawa	Ottawa, Ontario
Pennsylvania	P	University of Pennsylvania	Philadelphia, Pennsylvania
Pennsylvania State	S	Pennsylvania State University	University Park, Pennsylvania
Pittsburgh	S	University of Pittsburgh	Pittsburgh, Pennsylvania
Princeton	P	Princeton University	Princeton, New Jersey
Purdue	S	Purdue University	West Lafayette, Indiana

Institution	Category	Full Name of Institution	Location
Queen's	C	Queen's University	Kingston, Ontario
Rice	P	Rice University	Houston, Texas
Rochester	P	University of Rochester	Rochester, New York
Rutgers	S	Rutgers University	New Brunswick, New Jersey
Saskatchewan	C	University of Saskatchewan	Saskatoon, Saskatchewan
South Carolina	S	University of South Carolina	Columbia, South Carolina
Southern California	P	University of Southern California	Los Angeles, California
Southern Illinois	S	Southern Illinois University	Carbondale, Illinois
SUNY-Albany	S	University at Albany, State University of New York	Albany, New York
SUNY-Buffalo	S	University at Buffalo, State University of New York	Buffalo, New York
SUNY-Stony Brook	S	Stony Brook University, State University of New York	Stony Brook, New York
Syracuse	P	Syracuse University	Syracuse, New York
Temple	S	Temple University	Philadelphia, Pennsylvania
Tennessee	S	University of Tennessee	Knoxville, Tennessee
Texas	S	University of Texas	Austin, Texas
Texas A&M	S	Texas A&M University	College Station, Texas
Texas Tech	S	Texas Tech University	Lubbock, Texas
Toronto	C	University of Toronto	Toronto, Ontario
Tulane	P	Tulane University	New Orleans, Louisiana
Utah	S	University of Utah	Salt Lake City, Utah
Vanderbilt	P	Vanderbilt University	Nashville, Tennessee
Virginia	S	University of Virginia	Charlottesville, Virginia
Virginia Tech	S	Virginia Polytechnic Institute & State University	Blacksburg, Virginia
Washington	S	University of Washington	Seattle, Washington
Washington State	S	Washington State University	Pullman, Washington
Washington U.-St. Louis	P	Washington University	St. Louis, Missouri
Waterloo	C	University of Waterloo	Waterloo, Ontario
Wayne State	S	Wayne State University	Detroit, Michigan
Western	C	Western University	London, Ontario
Wisconsin	S	University of Wisconsin	Madison, Wisconsin
Yale	P	Yale University	New Haven, Connecticut
York	C	York University	North York, Ontario
Boston Public Library	N	Boston Public Library	Boston, Massachusetts
Center for Research Libraries	N	Center for Research Libraries	Chicago, Illinois
Library of Congress	N	Library of Congress	Washington, DC
National Agricultural Library	N	National Agricultural Library	Beltsville, Maryland
Natl. Archives & Records Ad.	N	National Archives & Records Administration	Washington, DC
National Library of Medicine	N	National Library of Medicine	Bethesda, Maryland
National Research Council Canada	X	National Research Council Canada, Knowledge Management	Ottawa, Ontario
New York Public Library	N	New York Public Library	New York, New York
New York State Library	N	New York State Library	Albany, New York
Smithsonian Institution	N	Smithsonian Institution	Washington, DC

S: US public university   P: US private university   N: US nonuniversity   C: Canadian university   X: Canadian nonuniversity

BIBLIOGRAPHY

PART A: Selected Articles from the ARL Newsletter

"The ARL Membership Criteria Index." *ARL: A Bimonthly Newsletter of Research Library Issues and Actions* no. 197 (April 1998): 9.

"Assessing ILL/DD Services: New Cost-Effective Alternatives." *ARL: A Bimonthly Report on Research Library Issues and Actions from ARL, CNI, and SPARC* no. 236 (October 2004): 9.

Askew Waller, Consuella, and Kaylyn Hipps. "Using LibQUAL+ and Developing a Culture of Assessment in Libraries." *ARL: A Bimonthly Report on Research Library Issues and Actions from ARL, CNI, and SPARC no.* 221 (April 2002): 10–11.

Carter, Lisa R. "Special at the Core: Aligning, Integrating, and Mainstreaming Special Collections in the Research Library." Research Library Issues: A Report from ARL, CNI, and SPARC no. 283 (October 2013): 1–5. http://publications.arl.org/rli283/1

Case, Mary M. "The Impact of Serial Costs on Library Collections." *ARL: A Bimonthly Report on Research Library Issues and Actions from ARL, CNI, and SPARC* no. 218 (October 2001): 9.

_____. "A Snapshot in Time: ARL Libraries and Electronic Journal Resources." *ARL: A Bimonthly Report on Research Library Issues and Actions from ARL, CNI, and SPARC no.* 235 (August 2004): 1–10.

Case, Mary M., and Judith Matz. "Framing the Issue: Open Access." *ARL: A Bimonthly Report on Research Library Issues and Actions from ARL, CNI, and SPARC* no. 226 (February 2003): 8–10.

Case, Mary M., and Prudence Adler. "Promoting Open Access." *ARL: A Bimonthly Report on Research Library Issues and Actions from ARL, CNI, and SPARC* no. 220 (February 2002): 1–5.

"Collections & Access for the 21st-Century Scholar: Changing Roles of Research Libraries." Report from the ARL Collections & Access Issues Task Force. *ARL: A Bimonthly Report on Research Library Issues and Actions from ARL, CNI, and SPARC* no. 225 (December 2002).

Cook, Colleen, Fred Heath, and Bruce Thompson. "A Brief LibQUAL+ Phase One Progress Report." *ARL: A Bimonthly Report on Research Library Issues and Actions from ARL, CNI, and SPARC* no. 219 (December 2001): 7.

Cook, Colleen, and Michael Maciel. "A Decade of Assessment at a Research-Extensive University Library Using LibQUAL+®." *Research Library Issues: A Bimonthly Report from ARL, CNI, and SPARC* no. 271 (August 2010): 4–12. http://publications.arl.org/rli271/6

Crow, Raym. "The Case for Institutional Repositories: A SPARC Position Paper." *ARL: A Bimonthly Report on Research Library Issues and Actions from ARL, CNI, and SPARC* no. 223 (August 2002): 1–4.

Crowe, William. "The End of History? Reflections on a Decade." *ARL: A Bimonthly Report on Research Library Issues and Actions from ARL, CNI, and SPARC* no. 226 (February 2003): 12–13.

Davidson, Catherine, and Martha Kyrillidou. "The Value of Electronic Resources: Measuring the Impact of Networked Electronic services (MINES for Libraries® at the Ontario Council of University Libraries." *Research Library Issues: A Bimonthly Report from ARL, CNI, and SPARC* no. 271 (August 2010): 41–47. http://publications.arl.org/rli271/43

Dowd, Jacqui. "LibQUAL+® and the "Library as Place" at the University of Glasgow." *Research Library Issues: A Bimonthly Report from ARL, CNI, and SPARC* no. 271 (August 2010): 13–20. http://publications.arl.org/rli271/15

"The Future of Human Resources in Canadian Libraries." *ARL: A Bimonthly Report on Research Library Issues and Actions from ARL, CNI, and SPARC* no. 240 (June 2005): 9.

Grosetta Nardini, Holly. "Building a Culture of Assessment." *ARL: A Bimonthly Report on Research Library Issues and Actions from ARL, CNI, and SPARC* no. 218 (October 2001): 11.

Groves, Richard. "Sharing Best Practices by Disseminating Assessment Results via the Web." *ARL: A Bimonthly Report on Research Library Issues and Actions from ARL, CNI, and SPARC* no. 236 (October 2004): 6.

Guedon, Jean-Claude. "Beyond Core Journals and Licenses: The Paths to Reform Scientific Publishing." *ARL: A Bimonthly Report on Research Library Issues and Actions from ARL, CNI, and SPARC* no. 218 (October 2001): 1–8.

Hahn, Karla. "The State of the Large Publisher Bundle: Findings from an ARL Member Survey." *ARL: A Bimonthly Report on Research Library Issues and Actions from ARL, CNI, and SPARC* no. 245 (April 2006).

Hipps, Kaylyn. "Diversity in the U.S. ARL Library Workforce." *ARL: A Bimonthly Report on Research Library Issues and Actions from ARL, CNI, and SPARC* no. 246 (June 2006): 1–2.

Johnson, Richard K. "Whither Competition?" *ARL: A Bimonthly Report on Research Library Issues and Actions from ARL, CNI, and SPARC* no. 217 (August 2001): 12–14.

Killick, Selena. "Service Quality Assessment with LibQUAL+® in Challenging Times: LibQUAL+® at Cranfield University." *Research Library Issues: A Bimonthly Report from ARL, CNI, and SPARC* no. 271 (August 2010): 21–24. http://publications.arl.org/rli271/23

Kyrillidou, Martha. "The ARL Library Scorecard Pilot: Using the Balanced Scorecard in Research Libraries." *Research Library Issues: A Bimonthly Report from ARL, CNI, and SPARC* no. 271 (August 2010): 33–35. http://publications.arl. org/rli271/35

_____. "ARL Statistics: Redefining Serial Counts and Remaining Relevant in the 21st Century." *ARL Newsletter: A Bimonthly Report on Research Library Issues and Actions from ARL, CNI, and SPARC* no. 262 (February 2009): 18–20. http://publications.arl.org/rli262/19

_____. "ARL University Libraries' Spending Trends." *ARL: A Bimonthly Report on Research Library Issues and Actions from ARL, CNI, and SPARC* no. 242 (October 2005): 10.

_____. "The Future of Librarians in the U.S. Workforce." *ARL: A Bimonthly Report on Research Library Issues and Actions from ARL, CNI, and SPARC* no. 246 (June 2006): 5.

_____. "The Impact of Electronic Publishing on Tracking Research Library Investments in Serials." *ARL: A Bimonthly Report on Research Library Issues and Actions from ARL, CNI, and SPARC* no. 249 (December 2006): 6–7.

_____. "LibQUAL+™ in 2004." *ARL: A Bimonthly Report on Research Library Issues and Actions from ARL, CNI, and SPARC* no. 236 (October 2004): 6.

_____. "Library Value May Be Proven, If Not Self-Evident." *Research Library Issues: A Bimonthly Report from ARL, CNI, and SPARC* no. 271 (August 2010): 1–3. http://publications.arl.org/rli271/3

_____. "Reshaping ARL Statistics to Capture the New Environment." *ARL: A Bimonthly Report on Research Library Issues and Actions from ARL, CNI, and SPARC* no. 256 (February 2008): 9–11.

_____. "Research Library Trends: A Historical Picture of Services, Resources, and Spending." *Research Library Issues: A Quarterly Report from ARL, CNI, and SPARC* no. 280 (September 2012): 20–28. http://publications.arl.org/rli280/20

_____. "Serials Trends Reflected in the ARL Statistics 2002–03." *ARL: A Bimonthly Report on Research Library Issues and Actions from ARL, CNI, and SPARC* no. 234 (June 2004): 14–15..

Kyrillidou, Martha, and William Crowe. "In Search of New Measures." *ARL: A Bimonthly Newsletter of Research and Library Issues and Actions* no. 197 (April 1998): 8–10.

Kyrillidou, Martha, and Kaylyn Hipps. "Symposium on Measuring Library Service Quality." *ARL: A Bimonthly Report on Research Library Issues and Actions from ARL, CNI, and SPARC* no. 215 (April 2001): 9–11.

Lippincott, Sarah, and Martha Kyrillidou. "How ARL University Communities Access Information: Highlights From LibQUAL+™." *ARL: A Bimonthly Report on Research Library Issues and Actions from ARL, CNI, and SPARC* no. 236 (October 2004): 7–8.

Lowry, Charles. "ARL Library Budgets after the Great Recession, 2011-2013." *Research Library Issues: A Report from ARL, CNI, and SPARC* no. 282 (June 2013): 1–12. http://publications.arl.org/3p33q9/rli282/2

Lynch, Clifford. "Institutional Repositories: Essential Infrastructure for Scholarship in the Digital Age." *ARL: A Bimonthly Report on Research Library Issues and Actions from ARL, CNI, and SPARC* no. 226 (February 2003): 1–7.

"Making Library Assessment Work." *ARL: A Bimonthly Report on Research Library Issues and Actions from ARL, CNI, and SPARC no.* 240 (June 2005): 9.

Mays, Regina, Carol Tenopir, and Paula Kaufman. "Lib-Value: Measuring Value and Return on Investment of Academic Libraries." *Research Library Issues: A Bimonthly Report from ARL, CNI, and SPARC* no. 271 (August 2010): 36–40. http://publications.arl.org/rli271/38

Potter, William Gray, Colleen Cook, and Martha Kyrillidou. "ARL Profiles: Qualitative Descriptions of Research Libraries in the Early 21st Century." *Research Library Issues: A Bimonthly Report from ARL, CNI, and SPARC* no. 271 (August 2010): 25–32. http://publications.arl.org/rli271/27

Shim, Wonsik "Jeff", Charles McClure, and John Carlo Bertot. "Measures and Statistics for Research Library Networked Services: ARL E-Metrics Phase II Report." *ARL: A Bimonthly Report on Research Library Issues and Actions from ARL, CNI, and SPARC no.* 219 (December 2001): 8–9.

Stuber, Peter. "Where does the Free Online Scholarship Movement Stand Today?" *ARL: A Bimonthly Report on Research Library Issues and Actions from ARL, CNI, and SPARC* no. 220 (February 2002): 9–15.

Unsworth, John M. "The Crisis in Scholarly Publishing in the Humanities." *ARL: A Bimonthly Report on Research Library Issues and Actions from ARL, CNI, and SPARC* no. 228 (June 2003): 1–4.

Vetter, Matthew and Sara Harrington. "Integrating Special Collections into the Composition Classroom: A Case Study of Collaborative Digital Curriculum." *Research Library Issues: A Report from ARL, CNI, and SPARC* no. 283 (October 2013): 16–20. http://publications.arl.org/rli283/16

Wetzel, Karen, and Mary Jackson. "Portal Functionality Provided by ARL Libraries: Results of an ARL Survey." *ARL: A Bimonthly Report on Research Library Issues and Actions from ARL, CNI, and SPARC no.* 222 (June 2002): 7–9.

Wilder, Stanley. "New Hires in Research Libraries: Demographic Trends and Hiring Priorities." *ARL: A Bimonthly Report on Research Library Issues and Actions from ARL, CNI, and SPARC* no. 221 (April 2002): 5–8.

Young, Mark. "*ARL Salary Survey* Highlights." *ARL: A Bimonthly Report on Research Library Issues and Actions from ARL, CNI, and SPARC* no. 246 (June 2006): 4.

PART B: Related Books and Articles Published in Other Sources

Arms, William. "Quality Control in Scholarly Publishing on the Web." *The Journal of Electronic Publishing* 8, no. 1 (August 2002). http://quod.lib.umich.edu/j/jep/3336451.0008.103/--what-are-the-alternatives-to-peer-review-quality-control?rgn=main;view=fulltext

Band, Jonathan. "The Three P's: A Tribute to Duane Webster." *portal: Libraries and the Academy* 9, no. 3 (July 2009): 367–74. http://muse.jhu.edu/journals/portal_libraries_and_the_academy/toc/pla.9.3.html

Baumol, W. J., and M. Marcus. *Economics of Academic Libraries*. Washington, DC: American Council of Education, 1973.

Bertot, John Carlo, Charles McClure, and Joe Ryan. *Statistics and Performance Measures for Public Library Networked Services*. Chicago: American Library Association, 2001.

Blixrud, Julia. "The Association of Research Libraries Statistics and Measurement Program: From Descriptive Data to Performance Measures." *Proceedings from the 4th Northumbria International Conference on Performance Measurement in Libraries and Information Services*, edited by Joan Stein, Martha Kyrillidou, and Denise Davis. Washington, DC: Association of Research Libraries, 2002.

Bowlby, Raynna. "Living the Future: Organizational Performance Assessment." *Journal of Library Administration* 51, no. 7–8 (October 2011): 618–44. http://www.arl.org/storage/documents/publications/bowlby-organizational-performance-assessment-5-31-11.pdf

Branin, Joseph J. "Duane Webster's Contributions to Leadership Development in Research Libraries, 1970–2008." *portal: Libraries and the Academy* 9, no. 3 (July 2009): 349–54. http://muse.jhu.edu/journals/portal_libraries_and_the_academy/toc/pla.9.3.html

Carlson, Scott. "The Deserted Library: As Students Work Online, Reading Rooms Empty Out – Leading Some Campuses to Add Starbucks." *The Chronicle of Higher Education*, November 16, 2001.

Case, Mary M. "Scholarly Communication: ARL as a Catalyst for Change." *portal: Libraries and the Academy* 9, no. 3 (July 2009): 381–96. http://muse.jhu.edu/journals/portal_libraries_and_the_academy/toc/pla.9.3.html

Clapp, V. W. *The Future of the Research Library*. Urbana: University of Illinois Press, 1964.

Coffman, Steve. "Building Earth's Largest Library: Driving into the Future." *Searcher* 7, no. 3 (March 1999).

Competition Commission of the United Kingdom. *Reed Elsevier, PLC, and Harcourt General, Inc.: A Report on the Proposed Merger*, presented to Parliament by the Secretary of State and Trade and Industry by Command of Her Majesty, July 2001.

Cook, Colleen, Fred Heath, Martha Kyrillidou, and Duane Webster. "The Forging of Consensus: A Methodological Approach to Service Quality Assessment in Research Libraries – the LibQUAL+ Experience." *Proceedings from the 4th Northumbria International Conference on Performance Measurement in Libraries and Information Services*, edited by Joan Stein, Martha Kyrillidou, and Denise Davis. Washington, DC: Association of Research Libraries, 2002.

Cook, Colleen, Fred Heath, and Bruce Thompson. "Score Norms for Improving Library Service Quality: A LibQUAL+ study." *portal: Libraries and the Academy* 2, no. 1 (January 2002): 13–26. http://muse.jhu.edu/journals/portal_libraries_and_the_academy/toc/pla2.1.html

Cook, Colleen, Fred Heath, Bruce Thompson, and Russell Thompson. "LibQUAL+: Service Quality Assessment in Research Libraries." *IFLA Journal* 27, no. 4 (2001): 264–68. http://archive.ifla.org/V/iflaj/art2704.pdf

———. "The Search for New Measures: The ARL LibQUAL+Project—A Preliminary Report." *portal: Libraries and the Academy* 1, no. 1 (January 2001): 103–12. http://muse.jhu.edu/login?auth=0&type=summary&url=/journals/portal_libraries_and_the_academy/v001/1.1cook.pdf

Cook, Colleen, Fred Heath, Bruce Thompson, and Duane Webster. "LibQUAL+™ Preliminary Results from 2002." *Performance Measurement and Metrics* 4, no. 1 (2003): 38–47. http://www.emeraldinsight.com/journals.htm?issn=1467-8047&volume=4&issue=1

Council on Library and Information Resources. *A Different Approach to the Evaluation of Research Libraries.* Research Brief 6. Washington, DC: The Council, 1998.

Cronenwett, Philip N., Kevin Osborn, Samuel A. Streit, eds. *Celebrating Research: Rare and Special Collections from the Membership of the Association of Research Libraries.* Washington, DC: Association of Research of Libraries, 2007.

Cummings, Anthony M., et al. *University Libraries and Scholarly Communication: A Study Prepared for The Andrew W. Mellon Foundation.* Washington, DC: Association of Research Libraries, 1992. http://catalog.hathitrust.org/Record/002625238

Cummings, M. M. *The Economics of Research Libraries.* Washington, DC: Council on Library Resources, 1986.

Dewey, Barbara I. "The Imperative for Diversity: ARL's Progress and Role." *portal: Libraries and the Academy* 9, no. 3 (July 2009): 355–62. http://muse.jhu.edu/journals/portal_libraries_and_the_academy/toc/pla.9.3.html

Downs, Robert B. "The Growth of Research Collections." *Library Trends: American Library History: 1876–1976* 25 (July 1976): 55–80.

———. "Uniform Statistics for Library Holdings." *Library Quarterly* 16 (January 1946): 63–69.

Drake, Miriam A. "Forecasting Academic Library Growth." *College and Research Libraries* 37, no. 1 (January 1976): 53–59.

Franklin, Brinley. "Duane Webster, Assessment Pioneer." *portal: Libraries and the Academy* 9, no. 3 (July 2009): 339–48. http://muse.jhu.edu/journals/portal_libraries_and_the_academy/toc/pla.9.3.html

Franklin, Brinley, Colleen Cook, Martha Kyrillidou, and Bruce Thompson. "Library Investment Index—Why Is It Important?" *Proceedings of the 2008 Library Assessment Conference: Building Effective, Sustainable, and Practical Assessment,* August 4–7, 2008, Seattle, Washington. (Washington, DC: Association of Research Libraries, 2009): 147–54.

Frazier, Kenneth. "The Librarians' Dilemma: Contemplating the Costs of the 'Big Deal,'" *D-Lib Magazine* 7, no. 3 (March 2001) http://www.dlib.org/dlib/march01/frazier/03frazier.html

Funk, Cara J. "ARL and Association 3.0: Ten Management Challenges." *portal: Libraries and the Academy* 9, no. 3 (2009): 405–10. http://muse.jhu.edu/journals/portal_libraries_and_the_academy/toc/pla.9.3.html

Gooden, Paul, Matthew Owen, and Sarah Simon. *Scientific Publishing: Knowledge is Power.* New York: Morgan Stanley, 2002.

Guthrie, Kevin M. "It Didn't Have to Be This Way: Entrepreneurship at ARL During Duane Webster's Tenure." *portal: Libraries and the Academy* 9, no. 3 (July 2009): 411–18. http://muse.jhu.edu/journals/portal_libraries_and_the_academy/toc/pla.9.3.html